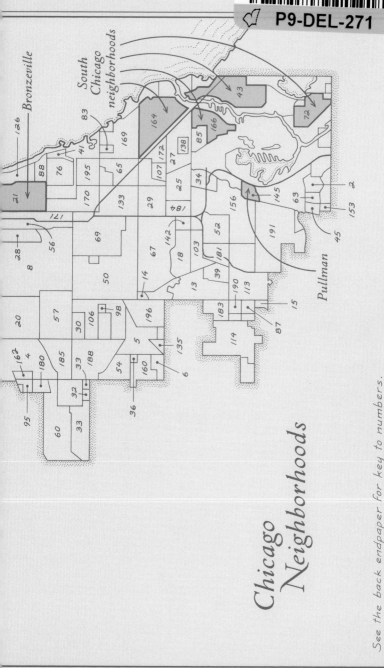

Chicago Neighborhoods

See the back endpaper for key to numbers.

Never a City So Real

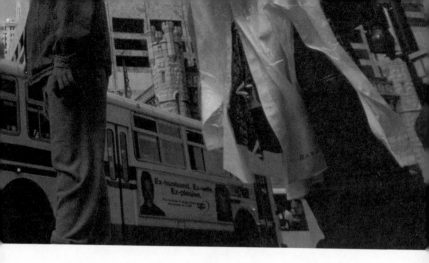

Never a City So Real

A WALK IN CHICAGO

Alex Kotlowitz

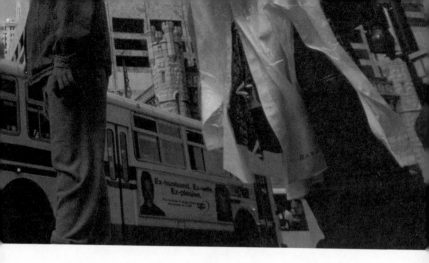**CROWN JOURNEYS**

CROWN PUBLISHERS · NEW YORK

Grateful acknowledgment is made to Donadio & Olson, Inc., *for permission to reprint an excerpt from* Chicago: City on the Make *by Nelson Algren. Copyright © 1951 by Nelson Algren. Reprinted by permission of Donadio & Olson, Inc.*

Published by Crown Journeys, an imprint of Crown Publishers, New York, New York
Member of the Crown Publishing Group, a division of Random House, Inc.
www.crownpublishing.com

CROWN JOURNEYS *and the Crown Journeys colophon are trademarks of Random House, Inc.*

Printed in the United States of America

Design by Lauren Dong
Title page photograph © Sandy Felsenthal/CORBIS
Map by Jackie Aher
Map source: City 2000

Library of Congress Cataloging-in-Publication Data
Kotlowitz, Alex.
Never a city so real : a walk in Chicago / Alex Kotlowitz.—1st ed.
1. Chicago (Ill.)—Social life and customs. 2. Chicago (Ill.)—Biography.
3. Chicago (Ill.)—Description and travel. I. Title.
F548.3.K68   2004
977.3'11–dc22   2004002860

ISBN 1-4000-4621-1

10   9   8   7   6   5   4   3   2   1

First Edition

For Mattie and Lucas

CONTENTS

Never a City So Real

My FATHER-IN-LAW, JACK WOLTJEN, SOLD EUCA-lyptus oil. He hawked it in two-ounce bottles at flea markets and county fairs. He took orders over the phone and then the Internet, and convinced local health stores to carry it. And he handed out samples to friends and strangers alike, including to his neighbors and the UPS man.

Jack named the oil, which was extracted from an Australian eucalyptus tree, V-Vax, derived from the Latin word *vivax*, which means tenacious for life. He believed it soothed bee stings and burns, that it cured everything from the common cold to kidney stones; he was also convinced that it helped slow the progress of AIDS. A confident, easygoing man who rarely got flustered, Jack could—and did—persuade almost everyone he met of V-Vax's curative properties. My wife, to this day, uses it for cold sores. Because the medicinal oil would eat through plastic, Jack had to package it in glass bottles. But he made a point of telling anyone who'd listen that he drank the stuff. Every morning, he poured a few drops into his orange juice. "I down it like a shot of whiskey, just like John Wayne," he once told a reporter for a local weekly.

Chicago, after all, is a place of passion and hustle, or as the early explorer René-Robert Cavelier, sieur de La Salle, wrote: "The typical man who grows up here must be an enterprising man. Each day as he rises he will exclaim, 'I act, I move, I push.'" And so my wife's father was celebrated here, for his entrepreneurial spirit and for his unwavering belief in himself. One of Jack's longtime friends told me, "I was never completely convinced of the healing power of V-Vax, but Jack was such a strong and caring person, and he never seemed to have any doubt that just his touch would have a healing effect, eucalyptus oil or not. He used to persuade elderly women that V-Vax had restorative powers. He didn't do this disrespectfully—he really believed it. He wasn't conning anyone. He said the women loved the feel of it on their hands."

Jack was a ruggedly handsome man, and I can easily imagine those elderly women swooning over him. At six foot two, he was built like an oak, firm and straight-backed. Even into his seventies, he ran five miles a day. He had an open and empathic face, and more often than not he was in high spirits. He also had an uncanny ability to make everyone feel as if he shared a special intimacy with them. Even when Jack got angry, which was usually out of indignation rather than due to some personal slight, his eyes still flickered with a measure of mischievousness.

Jack did things his way. He hung posters of paintings by the masters in his house, and while he thought that these works were good, they weren't as good as they could be. In a Matisse, he whited out a line he thought didn't belong. In a Gauguin, he added a cat. Just about all Jack listened to was Pink Floyd, and at his funeral, his children played *The Wall* on a boombox, much to the priest's dismay.

Jack, who died in 1999, personified the city, a place eternally in transition, always finding yet another way to think of itself, a city never satisfied. It's a city marked by its impermanence, though unlike, say, Los Angeles, which is regularly scorched and scarred and shattered by natural forces, Chicago's metamorphoses are generally shaped by human hands, the Great Fire of 1871 notwithstanding. It's a practical place—a city of necessity—where man has actually beaten nature. In 1900, for instance, when it became apparent that the sewage flowing from the Chicago River into Lake Michigan might contaminate the drinking water, the city simply reversed the flow of the river.

Jack loved the city for its ingenuity, as well as for its easygoing demeanor. "I can't see why anyone would want to live anywhere else in the world," he used to say. And he relished its tussles, large and small. He hustled, peddling his V-Vax, embracing the underdog, finding ways to reinvent himself—not for the purpose of self-aggrandizement, but rather because life is short and sometimes another path seems enticing and just worth the try.

Jack was born in Chicago, where he spent much of his youth (minus some years in Green Bay, Wisconsin). Raised a devout Catholic, in his twenties he entered Gethsemani, a Trappist monastery in the blue hills of Kentucky. His novice master was the theologian and author Thomas Merton. Gethsemani required a vow of silence, and at dinner if you wanted salt, you had to stare hard at the shaker until another brother noticed. One day, cutting down a tree, Jack couldn't contain himself. He held his head back and roared, "Timber." After that, his days at the monastery were numbered. Within a couple of years, he had married, and he and his young wife, Fran, who herself had just spent a year in a nunnery, opened a Catholic Worker farm in eastern Missouri for recovering alcoholics.

Jack and Fran eventually had nine children together, and found their way back to Chicago, where they settled in Austin, a neighborhood at the city's farthest western reaches, a collection of wood-framed single-family homes and grand-looking churches. The eleven of them lived in a three-bedroom home with one bathroom. Shortly after they moved in, in 1965, the complexion of Austin changed virtually overnight. As black families began buying into the neighborhood, realtors, in a scheme that became known as "blockbusting," deliberately frightened whites into selling. Blockbusting was a rather simple yet utterly destructive tactic. First, a realtor would buy a home on an all-white street, and move in a black family. Then, the white families on the block would panic, selling their homes to the realtor at bargain-basement prices. The realtor would then make a hefty profit by turning around and selling them to more black families. But Jack and Fran insisted on staying in Austin, and they made a show of it, joining civil rights marches through Chicago's segregated neighborhoods.

My wife remembers one rally her father took her to, where, at the age of ten, she clutched Ralph Abernathy's hand, trying to hide her face from her best friend's father, who was screaming racial epithets at the marchers from the curb. "Go-a back-a where you came from," the angry refugees from Eastern Europe's communism yelled at the blacks, refugees themselves from the Jim Crow south. This city is the story of newcomers, the Irish, Poles, Croats and Serbs, Mexicans, and more recently Asians and Africans, but in the end it's defined by race, by a history that is by turn ugly and celebratory, from the 1919 race riots to the 1983 election of the city's first black mayor, Harold Washington. Even milestones such as Washington's election come at a cost, though; it was marked by the ugliest and most divisive of campaigns, in which Washington's opposition rallied voters with the slogan, "Before It's Too Late."

In the 1960s and '70s, white landlords wouldn't rent to blacks. Jack didn't think that was right. And so he did what he could to force their hand. Working for a local fair-housing organization, Jack invented "testing"—a benign appellation, given the ugliness it uncovered. A black couple would try to rent an apartment and inevitably be turned down. Then Jack and a colleague posing as his wife would try to rent the same place, usually successfully. A lawsuit would follow. Among the white parents in the neighborhood Jack became known as "the underground spy for the spooks," an accusation he was perfectly comfortable with.

Jack eventually gave up that work to sell his V-Vax, as well as a lens cleaner that he liked to boast was used by NASA. Jack and Fran divorced in 1975, and a few years later, he and his new wife bought a three-flat on Elston Avenue, along the Chicago River. (Long before it was popular, Jack would launch his wood canoe from the riverbank nearby, pushing past the used condoms and floating beer bottles. Today, it's considerably cleaner and you can rent not only canoes but, no kidding, gondolas.) Jack bottled the V-Vax in his garage, running feeder tubes down from twenty-five steel drums that he stored on the second floor of his home. On holidays, the family would gather at the house on Elston Avenue, and Jack would regale us with stories of his antics, most of which we knew by heart.

Jack always, it seemed, pursued oversized ventures. Once the columnist Mike Royko held a kite contest along Lake Michigan, and Jack built one so large that the string tore the skin from his children's hands. (My wife remembers her father planning to use the kite to tow his canoe across the lake, but she can't recall whether, in fact, he ever tried it.) Another time, he hooked up the family's Alaskan malamute, Michi, to a sled he built, and had him pull two of the girls. He was so proud of this achievement that he called the *Chicago Daily News,* which ran a photo on its front page. Jack liked to boast that he was the one who first raised questions about the killing of the Black Panthers' twenty-one-year-old Fred Hampton and twenty-two-year-old Mark Clark. On December 4, 1969, thirteen policemen stormed the young men's West Side home. The police contended that the Panthers had opened fire on them, inviting newspaper reporters to take pictures of the bullet holes that had allegedly come from the Panthers' firearms. The police, undoubtedly feeling cocky about their conquest, kept Hampton's home open; in the following days, lines of people paraded through the apartment, including Jack—who, upon examining the contour of the "bullet holes," realized they'd been made by a hammer and nail. Jack said it was he who alerted the newspapers, and, indeed, a subsequent FBI investigation found that the Panthers had fired one bullet whereas the police had fired as many as ninety-nine.

On occasion, I'll be somewhere, and it'll come up in conversation that I'm married to a Woltjen. "Jack's daughter?" they'll ask. I'll tell them yes, and they'll smile and inevitably pass along some story. "He was," said a friend of his, "one of a kind."

When Jack's wife sold their house after his death, my wife decided she wanted only one item: a sculpture her father had erected in his side yard. Its design is simple: an anvil hanging by a thin cable from a tall wooden pole floats a foot above a metal dish filled with bird seed. I suppose that my wife has plans to reconstruct it in our backyard someday. I'm not sure—I'm afraid to ask. Jack once told a reporter, "When the birds come, they kind of look up nervously at the anvil while they eat. I think it's a beautiful juxtaposition of power and fragility." The same might be said of his chosen city.

CHICAGO IS A STEW of contradictions. Coarse yet gentle. Idealistic yet restrained. Grappling with its promise, alternately cocky and unsure. Nelson Algren—himself a bar of discordant notes—wrote in his prose poem, *Chicago: City on the Make,* "Once you've come to be a part of this particular patch, you'll never love another. Like loving a woman with a broken nose, you may well find lovelier lovelies. But never a lovely so real." An imperfect place, Chicago is America's city; it dreams America's dream.

Chicagoans, it has been said, are tribal, living among their own, a city of insiders whose entire identity is wrapped up in their neighborhood or parish. (I once asked the chief judge at criminal court where he was from, and he replied "Lady of Lords" as if that would assist me in placing him.) The former chief of staff for the city's current mayor once laughingly told me that he never felt a part of the City Hall gang because, as they would frequently remind him, he wasn't from Bridgeport, the southwest neighborhood where the mayor and his cronies hailed from. Indeed, Rand McNally sells one poster-size map that breaks the city into 198 neighborhoods (it's over 200 if you count a few it missed), each defined by ethnicity, race, or class, each distinct from the other, some with straight-forward designations like Ukrainian Village, Greektown, and Andersonville. A. J. Liebling, in a series of *New Yorker* pieces on the city in the 1950s, mistook this small-town quality for provincialism. He derisively referred to Chicago as "the Second City." Contrary to popular perception (and Liebling's claims) Chicagoans didn't take offense. In fact, eight years later, the city's premier comedy troupe—which spawned the likes of John Belushi, Joan Rivers, and Bill Murray—adopted the name, which has become a sort of rallying cry. One longtime newspaper columnist here recently said of Chicago's "Second City" status, "We don't give a fuck. We like it." Chicagoans are also a succinct people.

For all of Chicago's reputation as an insular place, it has, in fact, been molded if not defined by outsiders, people whose unconventionality flourished because there was no one to tell them to operate any other way. It's why Frank Lloyd Wright and Louis Sullivan changed the face of American architecture in Chicago and not in, say, Boston or New York. It's why Montgomery Ward and Sears-Roebuck formed their catalogue companies here, transforming rural America. And it's why Jane Addams, Ida B. Wells, and Saul Alinsky were able to raise hell, and in doing so push us to rethink the place of the dispossessed. It's a city that doesn't presume. It's a democratic city. Expansive and exposed. There's nothing false about it, no pretense. It is as you see it. Richard Wright, the author of *Native Son,* wrote that "it steals, helps, gives and cheats," and does so with more zest than any other city in the world. (Wright also wrote that Chicago is "the known city," suggesting that it had been examined and scrutinized, talked about and considered more than any other modern-day metropolis, which makes writing about it somewhat daunting.)

I'm an accidental Chicagoan. I grew up in New York, a city that thinks it's the center of the universe, which it is. I never felt that I truly belonged to New York. It's a place obsessed with status. Money. Beauty. Power. It's how you're measured there. Everybody, though, finds a place in Chicago. People are taken for who they are, not for what they have or haven't achieved. This is, after all, a city first settled by people running from failure or pursuing a buck; it's America's original pioneer town. As historian Donald L. Miller points out in his book *City of the Century,* when Chicago was first settled in the early 1800s, it was a mud hole, a windswept prairie marsh so inhospitable that the Miami Indians chose to settle elsewhere. The original settlers were, writes Miller, "rogues and roustabouts." Then the hundred-mile-long Illinois and Michigan Canal Corridor was completed in 1848, connecting Lake Michigan to the Mississippi River, and the city became the nation's

center of commerce, luring land and commodities speculators as well as builders of railroads, factories, and stock-
yards. Chicago soon became the destination for a cascade
of immigrant groups, and in the twentieth century the
terminus for African-Americans fleeing the South and for
farm boys looking to earn a living butchering hogs or
rolling steel.

I came here because as a journalist I thought it would
be a good perch from which to peer into America's heart,
but I didn't expect to find a home here. I expected to stay a
year, maybe two. It's been twenty, and counting.

The Italian sociologist Marco d'Eramo writes,
"Chicago expresses the truth about the United States."
Which truths, then, have I chosen to include here? I'm
going to admit right up front: This is a skewed and incom-
plete view of the city. I won't pretend otherwise. When I
told fellow Chicagoans what I was doing, they each had
their notions about what should and shouldn't be included, and they'd grumble and grouse. Inevitably, they'd
say, "How can you write a book about Chicago, and not
write about . . . ?" Fill in the blank. Chicagoans are a pos-
sessive sort. They have set notions of how people ought to
think of their home. Some feel that if this book is to be
considered a source for visitors to Chicago, it ought to
include all the obvious sites: Buckingham Fountain, the
Magnificent Mile, Wrigley Field, the Garfield Park Con-

servatory, and the Loop (which is how Chicagoans refer to their downtown because it is encircled by the tracks of the elevated train system, the El). Others believe that it ought to revel in the flowering of the city. In the 1990s, Richard M. Daley, son of the Boss, the late mayor Richard J. Daley, planted three hundred thousand trees— honey locust, hackberry, linden, mountain ash, elm, syca-more, flowering pear, ash, and Norway and silver maples. In 1996, he traveled to Paris, fell in love with it, returned home, and had the city hang hundreds of flower boxes from lampposts and bridges. By the end of the decade, he had the park district each year sowing 544,000 plants, 9,800 perennials, 156,000 bulbs, and 4,600 shrubs. This city of big shoulders is beginning to look more like a city with curves.

Indeed, despite Chicago's reputation for grayness and grittiness, it's a beautiful metropolis, even regal in places, especially along its twenty-nine miles of shoreline, which is as much as San Francisco's. Lake Michigan allows the city to breathe. The original Mayor Daley, the Boss, once said, "What is Paris next to Chicago? Has Paris got Lake Michigan?" (What to make of the father's and son's obses-sions with this European center some four thousand miles away?) Those who haven't been here imagine a body of water that can be easily encompassed by the eye, like a Maine lake or an ocean bay. But Lake Michigan is mon-strous. It's 333 miles from Chicago to the northernmost point, the Mackinac Bridge. It's 1,100 feet deep in places.

It's shared by four states. Some days, it can be as calm and inviting as a high society hostess; I've gone swimming off the rocks at night, and have bodysurfed when the winds are just right. But it can also be as rough and full of trickery as a three-card monte tosser. In an incident that upended my wife's family, one of her brothers, Johnny, drowned in Lake Michigan at the age of fourteen, knocked off his inflatable raft. The swells were so high, it took three days to recover his body.

However, this is not a book of lakes or flowers or buildings but rather of flesh and bone, of a place's people, its lifeblood. In one sense, I suppose, these portraits provide a street-level view of the city—a view from the ground up. On the other hand, none of the people you'll meet in these pages consider themselves at the bottom of anything. What most of them, including my father-in-law, do have in common, however, is that they look at their city from the vantage point of outsiders, and as a result they have perspective. They see things that you would miss if you were on the inside looking out. My friend Tony Fitzpatrick has a theory. Tony's an accomplished artist who produces exquisite, boisterous prints inspired by his experiences in the city. A big man, he has also been a Golden Gloves boxer and a character actor in both theater and film (usually tough guy or misfit roles). "People who don't fit in anywhere else fit in here," he says. "It's a collection of square pegs." Tony knows. He's lived in New York, in New Orleans, and in Saronno, Italy. "There was a twenty-year period I tried to leave Chicago," he explains. "But I kept coming back. I realized for better or worse that Chicago was the center of my compass. I loved it. I hated it. I understood it." And the city understood him, which is why the others you'll meet here have stayed as well. These are, in the end, people who give the city what one historian called its "messy vitalities."

Oil Can Eddie

Ten minutes now I have been looking at this.
I have gone by here before and wondered about it.
This is a bronze memorial of a famous general
Riding horseback with a flag and a sword and a
    revolver on him.
I want to smash the whole thing into a pile of junk to
    be hauled away to the scrap yard.
I put it straight to you,
After the farmer, the miner, the shop man, the factory
    hand, the fireman and the teamster,
Have all been remembered with bronze memorials . . .

Then maybe I will stand here
And look easy at this general of the army holding a
    flag in the air . . .

> CARL SANDBURG
> (from "Ready to Kill," *Chicago Poems*)

*F*OURTEEN MILES SOUTHEAST OF THE LOOP, AT THE base of Lake Michigan, the city's easternmost corner, one finds a fistful of neighborhoods with hearty names like Irondale, Hegewisch, The Bush, and Slag Valley. This is South Chicago. Apart from Altgeld Gardens—a vast public housing complex virtually hidden from the rest of the world by towering mountains of garbage and often referred to as Chicago's Soweto—South Chicago is the city's most isolated community, its most removed. The labor lawyer and author Tom Geoghegan has called it "a secret city." The vast majority of Chicagoans have never set foot here, and as if to ensure such detachment, above the compact redbrick bungalows with postage-stamp-size yards looms the Chicago Skyway, a highway on stilts, which takes the prosperous to their cottages along the Indiana and Michigan shorelines. The neighborhoods below are modest in appearance, a collection of small homes and small taverns and diners with simple names like Steve's, Pete's Hideaway, Who Cares?, Small World Inn, and Maria's Den. There's nothing fanciful about this area. As one observer wrote: "Streets named Commercial and Exchange offer testimony that people came here to make a buck, not admire the scenery."

And yet the scenery, so to speak, is awe-inspiring, the man-made equivalent of the Rockies. Dark, low-to-the-ground muscular structures, some three times the size of a football field, sprawl across the landscape, sprouting chimneys so tall that they're equipped with blinking lights to alert wayward aircraft. These chimneys shoot full-bodied flames thirty feet into the sky; at night they appear almost magical, like giant torches heating the moon. Billows of smoke linger in the air like phantom dirges. It used to be, when the steel mills were going strong, that these smokestacks spat out particles of graphite that would dust the streets and cars and rooftops like snow, catching the sun and setting the neighborhood aglitter. Suspended conveyor belts, pipes, and railroad overpasses weave in, out, and over the behemoth buildings. The noise is crushing, the stench of sulfur so powerful that not even a closed car window can keep it at bay. Had Rube Goldberg lost his sense of humor, this is, I imagine, what he would have produced.

This is the heart of American industrial might, or what's left of it. The first of the mills was built in the 1850s, and within a hundred years more steel was produced in this stretch of land than anywhere else in the world. The freighters delivered iron ore from Minnesota's Mesabi Range, and the mills turned the mineral into steel, shipping it west by rail and eventually east by the

St. Lawrence Seaway. By the 1960s, the mills employed eighty thousand men and women; they cascaded in from Poland, from Yugoslavia, from Mexico, and from the American South. Steel mills and refineries lined up along the dredged Calumet River and along the Lake Michigan shoreline, extending twenty-two miles from South Chicago to Gary, Indiana. This stretch of boiling steel was the equivalent of an industrial mountain stream, the source for can openers and knives, refrigerators and cars, bridges and skyscrapers. It fed this country's insatiable hunger for consumption and comfort. It was, in short, the nation's lifeblood.

The local population is still so dependent on the mills that the daily newspaper in Hammond, Indiana, which is just over the Chicago border, runs a box score every Wednesday of the region's steel tonnage and capacity. Nonetheless, there are only fifteen thousand working in the mills now; the owners grew complacent, so accustomed to their oligopoly that they forgot how to compete. Between the mills that still roll steel, there are hundreds of acres of vacant land littered with abandoned factory buildings stripped of their exteriors, brick coke houses collapsing in on themselves, and railroad tracks and bridges that have turned a muddy brown from rust.

ED SADLOWSKI, who is a sixty-four-year-old resident of South Chicago and who loves his city's opera, its museums, and its baseball teams, can't understand why his wife wants to move to Florida, where the world seems dipped in pastels. Sadlowski loves his neighborhood. Although he's been retired from the mills and from his union work for twelve years, he still feels most at home among its tired workers and its skeletal factories. He couldn't imagine living anywhere else. For him, the landscape of the past that connects him to his neighbors and to the world is palpable here, and Sadlowski fears that the story of his people might disappear if he were to abandon this place. He has become the custodian of its history.

I first became acquainted with Sadlowski in 1976, not in Chicago, but in a steelworkers' union hall in Bridgeport, Connecticut, when he was making labor history rather than fighting to preserve it. I was attending college nearby, where I eagerly detected rumblings of the coming class war in any worker who spoke derisively of his or her boss (which, I would later learn, included just about anyone who worked for someone else). Then I heard that this maverick, freespoken steelworker from Chicago was running for the international union's presidency, and that he actually had a chance. So a group of friends and I drove to Bridgeport and climbed the stairs to the second-floor meeting room where, despite our soft hands, long hair, and youth, we somehow thought we'd blend in. To be honest, I don't remember much of that gathering except for Sadlowski himself, who, dressed in an open-collared polyester shirt, was as eloquent and clearheaded a speaker as I'd ever heard. He talked of how the workers and the bosses have nothing in common. "It's a class question," he bellowed. I went away thinking that if this was the proletariat, I wanted in.

Sadlowski, who was a beefy man back then, has become beefier. (He once told a reporter while speaking of an eighty-seven-year-old friend who was physically fit: "He's as sharp as ever. I wonder what he drinks that keeps him that way." To which Sadlowski's wife, Marlene, replied, "Exercise!") He's always been a charismatic man—I've heard more than one woman say she had a crush on him—but his barrel of a belly now seems to rest precariously on his toothpick-thin legs. It's more, though, than just his physical bearing that's oversized. It's also his appetite for new people, new places, new ideas. His friends have included Studs Terkel and former presidential speechwriter Richard Goodwin. He's traveled throughout Europe, as well as to Russia, both for pleasure and to meet fellow trade unionists. His house is littered with books, mostly historical works on labor and war: on bookshelves, on tables, on the floor, in the basement, in the sun room. "Eddie's interests are omnivorous," says Tony Judge, a mutual friend. "He refuses to be limited by others' expectations of a labor guy. . . . He loves talk. He loves history. He'll talk to you about the Crimean War, about the Boer War, about Eskimos, about the union. He's an enormous furnace of a man who demands that those who come around him throw the door open and shovel like hell."

Age has been both cruel and kind to Sadlowski. He has had an operation for a brain tumor, which nips at his memory, and he's undergone three bypass surgeries. Over time, though, his features have softened, giving him a gentler look. He's still prone to say things that he knows will make others twitch with discomfort. His bushy eyebrows rise and fall with his pronouncements. Once, a labor reporter for the *Chicago Tribune* introduced himself to Sadlowski at a conference. "He looked at me," the reporter recounted for a local newsweekly, "and said 'How unusual. You never see prostitutes in the daylight.'" I had heard of this encounter, so when I introduced myself to Sadlowski at a gathering in Chicago, twenty-six years after I'd first heard him speak, I was careful to identify myself in the vaguest terms possible, as a "writer." I told him about sneaking into the union hall in Connecticut. His eyebrows rose like drawbridges. He leaned down. "Colonizer, huh," he said.

"Colonizer?" I asked.

"Which group were you with?"

I got it. It was how he referred to the steelworker wannabes, the young leftist sectarians who figured working in the mills would bring them closer to the revolution. "None," I stuttered.

"Man, thirty years that memory goes."

He patted me on the back, and laughed. What I later learned is that if, in fact, I had been a colonizer, it would have been okay by Sadlowski. At least, it would have meant I was on his side. And with Sadlowski, which side you're on still matters.

SADLOWSKI WAS SEVENTEEN when he first went to work for U. S. Steel at its South Works plant, a collection of more than a hundred buildings that covered an area nearly the size of New York's Central Park. It employed so many people—twenty thousand—that it sponsored a softball league of sixty-three teams. "When I went into high school, a counselor would steer you," he recalls. "He said, 'Sadlowski, you're assigned to industrial arts.' You know, wood shops, print shops, making shoeshine boxes, glass wind chimes, lamps out of old bowling pins. The whole point was that you were assigned to that with the thought that you were going to end up a worker in life, doing mechanical things." In his junior year (it's as far as he would get in school), a recruiter from U. S. Steel told an assembly of boys, "You can go there and get a trade, and no one can ever take a trade from you." Sadlowski didn't need much coaxing. His father, also named Ed, had become a millwright at Inland Steel after a stint as a semipro baseball shortstop, and although he discouraged the younger Ed from following him into the mills, he was his son's hero. Often during the summer, after the elder Sadlowski's shift ended near midnight, his son would meet him at the Plant 3 gate, and the two would drive to Calumet Fisheries, a takeout shack along the Calumet River (it still exists, and is worth a visit), where they'd order two pounds of deep-fried shrimp or sections of peppered smoked trout and pick up a six-pack of Meisterbrau. Then they'd wander down to the rocks along Lake Michigan, where they'd talk through the night—about baseball, about family, and about the union.

The younger Sadlowski's first job at the South Works plant was in the machine shop. The men called it "Happy Valley" because compared to places like the blast furnace, where temperatures topped one hundred fifty degrees, it was a fairly reasonable place to work. There Sadlowski oiled the prehistoric-looking machines—the lathes, the drill presses, and the hulking overhead cranes—and so earned the moniker "Oil Can Eddie."

"There was guys in the shop who done a lot of reading on the job," he says. "They'd be running a lathe, and it's gonna take an hour to go from here to there with the cutting tool, and they'd read a book. Management frowned on that, but guys did it. I'd read a book every couple of days. I'd go into the oil shanty away from the shop or into the locker room and sit in the toilet and read a book." Sadlowski read John Steinbeck and James T. Farrell, Upton Sinclair and John Dos Passos; in these novels he recognized himself and his fellow steelworkers, and the world began to make sense to him.

In 1959, Sadlowski married Marlene, who was at that time working as a dental assistant, and in four years they had four children. In 1962, he became a griever for the union. A griever is the union representative who takes workers' complaints to the boss, and for Sadlowski, there was never much of a gray area. "The company was the devil," he said. "Anyone who worked in the steel industry knew that—that the company wasn't no good." He learned the importance of good theater early on, and so made it a point to confront the foreman in his all-glass office where his coworkers could witness the exchange: the foreman sitting behind his desk with Sadlowski towering over him, gesticulating wildly, his hands slashing the air as if he were about to impart physical damage. "When they see that and they see that you produce, they'll follow you to hell," he told me.

Sadlowski rose fast in the union. First, he became president of his local, then he ran for the directorship of District 31, a consortium of the locals in the mills along the Chicago–Indiana corridor. The incumbent union machine, which called itself "the Official Family," had been in power for thirty years and wasn't about to relinquish its position easily. They refused, for instance, to give Sadlowski the location of all 285 locals, and so he, as well as family members and friends, dispersed throughout the city, looking for factories and then sneaking in to talk with the union members there. He lost the election, but it soon became clear that the Official Family engaged in massive voter fraud, filling out blank ballots—for their own family, of course. In a new election, which was monitored by four hundred federal observers, Sadlowski won by twenty thousand votes.

In 1976, at the age of thirty-seven, Sadlowski took on sixty-year-old Lloyd McBride for the presidency of the international union. The old guard, of which McBride was a part, had recently entered into a more cooperative arrangement with management. They had signed a contract that called for all disputes to be settled by arbitration. The union had promised not to strike, and I. W. Abel, who was stepping down as president of the union, had signed and let his picture be used in an industry newspaper ad pleading for higher productivity. Sadlowski saw things differently. His perspective harked back to labor's more militant days. He believed that there was a point at which the interests of management and that of the workers diverged. He believed it was a mistake for the union to give up its most powerful weapon. He believed that the members of the union should be allowed to vote on this new experimental contract. His campaign gathered momentum, and soon *Time* magazine warned that "if Sadlowski does become the Steelworkers' chief, both the economy and the climate of the nation's labor–management relations could be significantly affected." One company executive told a reporter that if Sadlowski was elected "it would be a whole new ballgame." (The executive also tipped his hat to Sadlowski, saying "He was far and away the ablest union guy who has come down this pike—dedicated, tireless, and honest.") Profiles of Sadlowski appeared in *Rolling*

Stone and *The New York Times Magazine*. He gave an interview to *Penthouse* and appeared on *Meet the Press*. He became the darling of the left; Richard Goodwin and the television producer Norman Lear held fund-raisers for him. Geoghegan, in his marvelous book *Which Side Are You On?*, wrote, "It's hard to believe now, but in 1976 this was a big story." Bigger for some, Geoghegan recounts, than the presidential election that year, between Jimmy Carter and Gerald Ford. Sadlowski became a modern-day paradox, a working-class hero in a country that doesn't think it has classes.

When the old guard accused Sadlowski of being a communist dupe, he told a *New York Times* writer: "You can make it sound like any kind of revolutionary rhetoric you want but the fact is it's the working class versus the coupon clipper. The boss is there for one damn purpose alone, and that is to make money, not to make steel, and it's going to come out of the worker's back. . . . I guess maybe I'm a romantic, but I look on the American labor movement as a holy crusade, which should be the dominant force in this country to fight for the workingman and the underdog and make this a more just society."

Sadlowski tapped a deep vein of worker discontent, and so faced deep hostility from the opposition. One Sadlowski supporter at a steelworkers' convention was beaten up by three old-line unionists. Another, while pamphleteering outside a Houston factory, was shot in the neck. (Marlene says the supporter resembled her husband from behind, and she believes that that's who they thought they were shooting.) In the end, Sadlowski lost the election, garnering forty-four percent of the vote. In hindsight, some say he should have waited—until he was older, until his politics had mellowed, until the world caught up with him. But Sadlowski was impatient, and not without reason, since he saw what was coming in America's heartland, a dismantling of people's livelihoods.

It wasn't easy for Sadlowski after the loss. He spent the next fifteen years working in various union staff jobs, and for some of that time drinking too much. ("I drank everything," he says.) "In the end," a friend observed, "he had to answer to guys who in every way were his inferiors, ham-and-egg guys, guys who should've been glad to hold his overcoat. They couldn't get rid of him, but they reduced him." He retired from the union in 1992, the same year that U. S. Steel shuttered South Works, where he had begun. But Sadlowski has brushed himself off and started again. He has stopped drinking and is now involved with labor and with his community in a new capacity, as a guardian of their histories.

A COUPLE OF YEARS AGO, our mutual friend Tony Judge suggested that I spend a day with Sadlowski. Tony, a kind of intellectual entrepreneur, is connected to just about everyone in the city, and once a year, the two men drive around Chicago and visit sites that mean something to

Sadlowski, like the gravesite of Allan Pinkerton, whose Pinkerton guards were frequently used to break strikes. Sadlowski, Tony told me, likes to urinate on Pinkerton's grave. "He sees the lineage stuff," Tony says. "The old grudges are his grudges." So, with Tony's introduction, I called Sadlowski, who growled and grumbled, and grudgingly agreed to meet.

We spent a day in Sadlowski's Ford Crown Victoria, which has nearly two hundred thousand miles on it, tooling around South Chicago ("Fucked-up nothingness," he says of the graveyard of factories and forges along the Calumet River). Then, a few weeks later, he invited me to attend a play about a long-ago strike, which he and fellow steelworkers had written and now performed, and then I tagged along with him to a lunch of fried chicken and sausage for pensioners, where the men played poker and talked about the prescription drugs they were taking, and the women, widows of steelworkers, tried their hand at bingo. These people still come to Sadlowski with their problems. Pension checks that are late. Health benefits not kicking in. Sadlowski, who often runs into his former coworkers from South Works over early-morning coffee at the local McDonald's, says of them, "I'm not romanticizing when I say this, but they're some of the sharpest guys I ever met in my life. They knew the score."

In fact, local history has been a bit more complicated than that. This is, after all, the same community that, over the course of seven months in 1953, threw rocks and bombs into the Trumbull Park low-rise public housing complex to keep blacks from moving in. It's also the same community that elected Ed Vrdolyak as its alderman for four consecutive four-year terms. In the 1980s, Vrdolyak led the white majority on a city council that reveled in its ability to block virtually every piece of legislation proposed by Harold Washington, who as Chicago's first black mayor was dismissed, if not reviled, by a portion of the city. But Sadlowski is a man of eternal faith. When looking, for instance, at something like the Trumbull Park experience, he points not to those who threw the projectiles but to the few courageous ones who challenged their friends and families to support the African-American family who moved in. (Sadlowski was also a big supporter of Harold Washington.) It's not blindness, just Sadlowski's inclination to buck the prevailing notion that the blue-collar worker in this country always shares the politics of Archie Bunker. "If you're a working stiff," he says, "your history becomes distorted."

Sadlowski now teaches a labor history class to carpenters and millwrights at a nearby Indiana college. "I just want to get them thinking about the working class," he tells me. "They don't even understand that there is such a thing." (He also was appointed to the Illinois Labor Relations Board, which helps resolve labor disputes involving public employees.) One Saturday morning, Sadlowski invites me to join him and his students, thirty-six men and one woman, for a field trip. All of them are in their twenties and early thirties, dressed in hooded sweatshirts and Carhartt jackets. Each has a cell phone on his (or her) belt. They wear baseball caps announcing their allegiances: Chicago Cubs, Bud King of Beers, Killian's, Rapala, and Rail Cats (a semipro baseball team that plays in a stadium called the Steel Yard). They look as if they'd rather be elsewhere, and early on, when Sadlowski, sitting in the front of the bus, starts rambling on about his days in the mills, a voice from the back hollers out, "Come on, Ed."

"What do you think their attention span is?" he mumbles. "Half a commercial?" But Sadlowski loves these guys. Their lives are constrained by what they know and by where they live, but they know enough to recognize that getting by with what skills they have may not cut it as the world turns, and so have elected to come back to school, to figure out what's next. (One tells me he wants to become a nurse.) They've also had the good fortune to run across Sadlowski, and Sadlowski the good fortune to run across them; they're cut from the same cloth, and Sadlowski can tell them whence that cloth came.

At Sadlowski's direction, the bus driver turns off Burnham Avenue, over the curb, and along a stretch of cracked cement that wends its way through a large field of tall weeds and prairie grass. A quarter of a mile in, Sadlowski tells everyone to get off the bus. According to Sadlowski, the nearby Calumet River was at one time the most industrialized waterway in the world. Now, as the carpenters and millwrights stand there, chilled by the early fall wind, he gestures toward the river and rattles off the names of the companies that once lined its banks: "Interlake Steel. Valley Mold and Iron. South Works. American Shipyard. Calumet Shipyard. Wisconsin Steel. Republic. Acme." It's to make a point. A few days earlier in class, one of his students had ripped into people living off the dole, people taking welfare handouts. "Too often, we point fingers," Sadlowski tells his students. "How can people live like that? I'll show you how it can be. Forty, fifty years working in a steelmill, doing what society expects of you, and then . . ." He claps his hands together. He has their attention.

"So where do the guys go?" a young carpenter by the name of Joe Gilmak asks.

"That's my point," Sadlowski says.

Sadlowski has taken his blue-collar protégés to this field because it's the site of the Memorial Day Massacre (not to be confused with the Valentine's Day Massacre, an Al Capone–ordered killing on the city's North Side); it's in places like this, Sadlowski tells them, that their lives and livelihoods are rooted. In 1937, the nascent steelworkers' union was attempting to win recognition at the smaller steel companies, and Republic Steel resisted, locking out its workers. The men and their families had gathered at a nearby tavern, Sam's Place, and decided to march on the company. As they approached the gates of the plant, Chicago policemen shot into the crowd, and then went after the strikers and their families with pickaxes supplied by the company. Ten men were killed, another eighty-four injured. It would be another five years before Republic recognized the union. Sadlowski takes his students across the street, to a former union hall (now a church-run community center), which still bears a plaque listing the victims and declaring them "Martyrs—Heroes—Unionists."

This is a city of plaques and monuments, a city with a long memory, for the famous and not-so-famous, for the virtuous and nonvirtuous. Sadlowski has also led a contingent of steelworkers to the burial grounds (in the suburb Forest Park) of the anarchists hanged because of their alleged role in the Haymarket Affair; a century later, it's a controversy that still rages. On May 4, 1886, a few hundred men and women gathered at a corner just west of downtown in support of workers locked out at the McCormick Harvester Works (two workers had been killed by the police the previous day), and as the crowd was breaking up, someone threw a bomb into the police lines, killing seven policemen. Eight activists, seven of them foreign-born, were convicted on flimsy evidence, and five were sentenced to death, partly at the insistence of business leaders including Marshall Field, the founder of the department store of the same name. Field also supplied the National Guard with Gatling guns and urged the construction of nearby Fort Sheridan to hold off any future uprisings. Despite protests from around the world, four of the anarchists were eventually hanged. (One killed himself before going to the gallows by biting down on a dynamite cap.) An estimated two hundred thousand people—a quarter of the city's population—lined the streets to view the funeral procession. Seven years later, at the urging of Clarence Darrow, Governor John P. Altgeld, the first foreign-born man chosen to lead the state, pardoned the men posthumously, to which the *Chicago Tribune* responded: "Governor Altgeld has apparently not a drop of pure American blood in his veins."

Three years after the Haymarket incident, the city erected a monument to the police officers who were killed by the bomb. Nearly a century later, in 1969, during the tumult of that time, someone placed a stick of dynamite between the legs of the bronze policeman, which toppled it. The city recast it. A year later, someone blew it up again. So the city placed a twenty-four-hour police guard at the statue, and when that proved too costly moved it to the courtyard of the Police Academy, where it stands today, well protected. Memories die hard here. As William Faulkner once said, "The past isn't dead; it isn't even past."

SADLOWSKI HERDS the students back on the bus and has the driver motor along the river, past what used to be Acme Steel; along the fence is a FOR SALE sign that notes the property's assets: "89 acres on Calumet River with dockage." In the distance is the blast furnace upon which the company had painted a large yellow smiley face. "You work on the fuckin' thing, it wasn't smiles," Sadlowski tells me. If there was a place close to hell, it was the blast furnace, where men would shovel coke and limestone into the furnace; it would get so hot that men had to wear asbestos-lined coats. During his 1976 campaign, Sadlowski had told the *Penthouse* interviewer that no one in this country should have to work in a coke oven, a place even harder on workers than the blast furnace; there, the tar was extracted from the coal, and noxious gases and fumes were spewed into the factory air. It was a remark that his opposition used in its campaign to suggest that Sadlowski would encourage plant closings. Sadlowski may be a romantic, but not about the work.

We then head west, across the river, to the preserved Pullman community, which at the end of the nineteenth century was built to be a workingman's paradise but soon became a workingman's prison. George Pullman made his money producing the Pullman Palace Car, the equivalent of a hotel on wheels. In 1880 he built the town, a collection of handsome brick townhouses with indoor plumbing, a luxury at the time. The town also had a European-style market square, an exquisite hotel (named after Pullman's daughter, Florence), and its own school and a church, which was meant to be shared by all denominations. Pullman's workers became unwitting participants in his ambitious—and misguided—social experiment.

During the recession of the 1890s, Pullman cut the wages of his workers, but their rents remained unchanged.

"He was a ruthless son of a bitch," Sadlowski tells his students. "But cunning. He'd cut the carpenters' wages two to five percent, and nobody would come to their aid. It's not me, they'd say. Then a few months later, he'd cut the tinsmiths two to five percent. Creating divisiveness among the workers. Some might ask why the workers didn't come together. Man doesn't work that way. Why do people react that way? A hope that it won't happen to them. But the unfortunate thing about man's reaction is he doesn't learn. Same goddamn thing today. That's a thing that should be taught in school, but it's the very schools that are teaching the bigwigs how to screw others."

In 1894, Sadlowski tells his students, the Pullman workers finally walked out on strike. Soon after, Eugene Debs's Railway Union honored the walkout, refusing to work on any train that carried a Pullman car, which was virtually every train in the country. It was a defining moment for American labor—an industrial union bringing together these otherwise fragmented crafts, undergirding the notion that an injury to one is an injury to all. Clarence Darrow, a young lawyer at the time for the Northwestern Railroad, stopped off in Pullman to see what all the fuss was about, and he became so moved by the plight of the immigrant workers there that he quit his job and offered his services to Debs and the union. (Each year on March 13, the anniversary of Darrow's death in 1938, Sadlowski gathers with others at the Jackson Park Lagoon in Hyde

Park, where Darrow's ashes were scattered; they read from his speeches and ruminate on matters of the day, as Darrow would have liked.)

Many lives were lost, and the strike was eventually smothered. When Pullman died, four years later, he was buried in the dead of night, in a hole the size of a large room. He had become so despised that he feared his grave would be desecrated, so he left instructions that his mahogany casket was to be buried in cement overlaid with bolted-down railroad ties. "He just got it into his head that someone would desecrate his body, maybe cut his penis off and stick it in his nose," Sadlowski tells me, making me wonder just how much he'd thought about this. Pullman is buried at the Graceland Cemetery, which, as Sadlowski says, "is as good a book as any on Chicago, and on the rich and how they thought of themselves." Marshall Field is buried there. So is Louis Sullivan, who died penniless and has a rather modest tombstone, although an elaborate monument was later built by friends.

As we're leaving the Pullman church, Gilmak, one of the students, admires the restoration work on the building's green limestone and thanks Sadlowski for the tour. Gilmak's grandfather worked at South Works, his dad at Republic, and his uncle at Wisconsin Steel. "Sadlowski," he told me later, "gave me more respect for those guys."

SADLOWSKI'S NEIGHBORHOOD, once largely Eastern European, is now mostly Mexican-American, a change that not all of the community's longtime members are happy about. Not long ago, when Sadlowski went to get a haircut, he told his longtime barber that he had just returned from visiting Tucson, Arizona.

"Yeah, they found a truckload of them spics in the desert there dead," the barber said. "Should've been fifty of the sonofabitches. We wouldn't have to bother with 'em then."

Sadlowski rose from his chair. "I come in here to get a haircut and I got to be subjected to that shit and pay for it? That's the same kind of crap they said about my grandfather a hundred years ago."

"It's nothing personal," the barber said.

"It's very personal to me." Sadlowski replied, and left without the haircut.

This, in the end, is what it's all about for Sadlowski: recognizing that, indeed, the past is present. It's easy to come down here and think to yourself, "This is a dying community," but it isn't. It's a changing one, now lined with establishments such as Armando's Tire Repair, D'Madera Furniture, Ruiz Funeral Homes, and Las Delicias Grocery. Like the carpenters and millwrights in Sadlowski's class, the neighborhood is picking itself up, brushing off the sulfur, and becoming something new.

Once while I was visiting his home, Sadlowski showed

me the rock garden he had created alongside his bungalow. It's a collection of stones and waste from the mills. There's a basketball-size mass of slag from South Works and a piece from another mill, Jones & Laughlin. He shows me a fist-size lump of coke from Acme and a paving stone from a street in South Chicago. There's a chunk of raw iron he found at the beach by South Works, where his dad and he used to sit, eat shrimp, drink beer and talk, and which is now being turned into a park.

Unexpectedly moved, I asked Sadlowski whether this rock garden was intended as a monument to what used to be. Sadlowski scowled.

"This isn't a monument to the fuckin' steel mills," he snapped. He placed a conciliatory hand on my shoulder and explained. "It's a way to enhance my memories of the guys who worked there—the comradeship, the decency, the knowledge I got from them. I owe everything I have to those people. Without them and without Marlene I'd be physically dead. I truly feel that way."

Millie and Brenda

I'M HAVING LUNCH AT MANNY'S, AN OLD-STYLE JEWISH delicatessen just south of the Loop, with two longtime friends, Mildred Wortham and Brenda Stephenson. Millie is impulsive and vocal, Brenda more cautious and even-tempered. They're always in full bloom, bedecked in colorful hip-hugging dresses in the summer, floppy hats and dazzling pantsuits in the winter.

Both of them grew up in Rockwell Gardens, a West Side public housing complex that in the 1980s had the dubious distinction of having the highest rate of murders, rapes, and assaults of any neighborhood in the city. They have since moved, though they still live on the West Side. For seventeen years, they have worked for a small organization, West Side Future, which assists young mothers in their early years of parenting. Brenda and Millie hand out diapers and toothbrushes (when I became a father, they loaded me down with gear as well), and pass along their wisdom. In a sense, they're professional busybodies. Once, I tagged along with Brenda as she was doing home visits; just as we were leaving the apartment of a nineteen-year-old mother, Brenda whipped around and demanded, "Are you pregnant?" "No way," the young woman replied. "Just thought I'd ask when your guard was down," laughed Brenda, who then kissed the teenager's son before skipping out the door.

On this particular day, as we're finishing our meal at Manny's, the two start giggling like little girls. Millie asks the question. Well, it's really more like a statement.

"So, Alex, I hear you got a little boy on the West Side."

I'm befuddled, not sure what or whom she's referring to.

Brenda says, "People say he looks just like you. Real soft-skinned. Curly hair."

"What are you talking about?" I ask. I laugh, nervously, which is probably not the best thing to do in the face of such a live rumor.

"C'mon, Alex," Millie says, putting her arm around my shoulder. "You can tell us. People say you got a boy by a girl you know'd on the West Side."

"You got to be kidding," I say.

"Yeah, and people say you don't go see him, or nothing."

I tell them that's simply not true—not that I don't see my son on the West Side, but that any such son exists.

"You can tell us," Brenda says.

"There's nothing to tell." My voice starts to rise. I know

I'm sounding a tad defensive. And though by the time we leave Manny's they tell me that they believe me, I'm not convinced they do. The next time we get together, Brenda pokes me in the ribs, winks, and asks how my boy is.

FOR FIFTEEN YEARS, Brenda, Millie, and I have been having lunch every couple of months—to gossip, to commiserate, to share stories, to catch up. Once, in the middle of lunch at Edna's, a soul food restaurant on the West Side, two beefy men sat down at the booth adjacent to ours. They interrupted our conversation and started flirting with Brenda and Millie. "Hey, babe, where you live?" one asked. "What you up to later?" The other man, who I later learned was a local minister, squeezed into the booth next to me, leaned over the table, and in a deep baritone voice complimented Brenda and Millie on their outfits. It was as if I wasn't there. I figured Brenda and Millie were enjoying it, but in fact they were furious on my behalf. Finally Brenda cut the man short, nodded toward me, and said in a level voice, "He's got us covered." Both men looked perplexed. They must have thought I was the luckiest man alive. When they left the restaurant, Brenda chastised me. "Next time," she said, "you tell them you got us covered. Hear me. Don't let nobody do you like that."

Brenda and Millie grew up in the same high-rise, just floors apart. When they were in their twenties, single and swinging, they'd each use the other's apartment as a place to take their dates. That way, they told me, men wouldn't know where they lived. The two are inseparable. They're good at sniffing out parties thrown by politicians, and on occasion they have dragged me along for the free food, and often good music and dancing. People often confuse them. "I'm called Millie all the time," Brenda says. Because Brenda is more reserved, Millie will often negotiate with men who want to ask her for a date. The two used to breakfast at Moon's, a working person's diner up the street from Rockwell Gardens, next to a post office. "We'd be sitting there and guys would come in, and they'd say to Millie, 'Who's your friend?' " Brenda recalls.

Millie laughs. "So I tell 'em, 'C'mon, let's get some coffee and breakfast, and I'll tell you about her.' "

"I wouldn't know a thing," says Brenda.

"And I'm telling her, 'Girl, order your breakfast, 'cause I know it's taken care of.' "

They can get a free ride anywhere in the city. Livery drivers will drop what they're doing to tote them from one place to another. Once, they got a lift home from a tavern in an ambulance, with sirens screaming; another time they hitched a ride in a hearse.

My friendship with Millie and Brenda revolves around food. It's what we do when we get together: eat. Millie's anxious because her son is on an aircraft carrier in the Middle East, so she calls, and we make lunch plans. Or I'm trying to get help for a young man I've known for years who I suspect is doing heroin, and so I call them. We make lunch plans.

Chicago is a mecca for some of the nation's finest chefs, but you'll learn more about the city itself from its neighborhood restaurants—those establishments where the food is served in heaps rather than manicured slivers, where, if you eavesdrop wisely or linger long enough, you can hear the stories of the neighborhood, of its people, of its legends and of its stresses and strains.

ONE DAY, over lunch at Manny's, Millie tells me of their encounter with a well-known pimp on the West Side named, uninventively, Don Juan. He wore emerald green suits and strutted around the neighborhood as if he owned all the women there. He once boasted to a local reporter that "in fifteen years only one of my girls ever got frost-bitten." He took a liking to Brenda, and one afternoon the two friends were traveling on the Madison Street bus, when Don Juan pulled up alongside in his emerald green Cadillac, first honking his horn, then pulling in front of the bus. Don Juan sent his driver on board; the man walked up to Brenda and said, "You ain't got to ride no bus, baby."

"I ain't going anywhere," Brenda told him. "I'm fine."

"C'mon, baby, your friend can come, too," he said, pointing to Millie.

Brenda turned her back on him.

Millie's telling me the story, laughing and shaking her head, and out of the corner of my eye, I catch an older gentleman at the next table clearly enjoying the yarn. He hurriedly buries his head in his newspaper.

Manny's seems to invite eavesdropping, in large part because of the medley of people it attracts. One weekday morning, I'm there for breakfast, and at one of the nearby Formica tables, four regulars—all elderly men—start passing around something I can't quite make out. One of them, a retired deputy police superintendent, is smoking a cigar. Another, who used to run a plumbing supply business, is doing all the talking. He's a short man with a big mouth. He appears to be showing his friends some trinkets he's hawking. He holds up a pacifier. When he shakes it, it lights up.

"Kids love 'em," he tells his friends.

"Cost a nickel apiece. Sell it for a buck ninety-nine. Not bad," one of them replies.

The retired plumbing supplier shrugs. "Cost me twenty cents," he says.

The former deputy police superintendent gets the pacifier to light up. "Cute," he says. "But how do you turn this thing off?"

"Got to squeeze it."

I'm sitting a few tables away with Manny's owner, Kenny Raskin, who looks over at the bearer of the pacifiers. "He's been banned from here twice," Raskin tells me. "He swears a lot and starts arguments with customers. But his brother convinced me to let him back in." Raskin shrugs. "Eh, I don't like to have enemies."

Indeed, over the years Manny's has become neutral turf. During one stretch in the late 1980s, Raskin recalls, there'd be a group of First Ward politicos seated at one table, many of whom were under investigation for organized crime, and then a group of plainclothed detectives from the organized crime unit sitting a few tables away. "They'd talk to each other," says Raskin. "They were friendly." Manny's is a political hangout, for politicians of all denominations, which in this fully Democratic city represents, some might say, the paragon of tolerance. On a recent election day, U.S. Senate candidate Dick Durbin brought his family here after he'd voted. Mayor Daley comes in occasionally (matzoh ball soup and corned beef sandwich), though he usually sends an aide to pick up his lunch. Harold Washington, when he was mayor, preferred the baked short ribs, and often he'd come in toward closing when the restaurant was empty to meet with constituents and advisers. The present governor, Rod Blagojevich, who lunches here regularly, signed his minimum-wage bill at Manny's. And the former governor, George Ryan, a Republican, came here for lunch when he was wrestling over whether to commute the sentences of death-row inmates. While he was chewing on his corned beef sandwich, his cell phone rang. It was Nelson Mandela, urging him to clear death row, which Ryan did the next day.

Manny's is in a neighborhood that used to be predominately Jewish, but that is now more commercial than residential. It's a quick cab ride from downtown, in a neighborhood of small clothing and shoe stores, just a few blocks away from the city's once bustling Maxwell Street Sunday market. It's been around since 1945, when Raskin's grandfather, Jack, opened Sonny's, which he soon changed to Manny's, after his son. When Jack died in 1993, his funeral procession received a large police escort because the then-chief-of-police (chicken noodle soup and grilled American cheese sandwich) was a regular customer. Raskin, who sports a goatee and mustache, has put on a bit of a paunch over the years, which he explains is due to his habit of "nibbling" in the kitchen. "You grab a potato pancake," he tells me, "or the corned beef, or take a piece of French bread and hollow it out and stuff it with a couple of meatballs." His favorite meals, he tells me, are the beef stew and oxtail stew, both original recipes from more than half a century ago.

A group of middle-aged women makes their way down the cafeteria line, ordering their breakfasts. Raskin gently waves. City inspectors, he tells me, gathering for their inspection of the newly rebuilt Soldier Field, the stadium where the Chicago Bears play. "I hate it," he says, " 'cause I feel like I'm under constant scrutiny." And, indeed, a few weeks later one of them had him adjust one of the sneeze guards on the service line.

A pacifier flies through the air, from the retired plumbing supplier to another friend. "What d'ya think?" the pacifier salesman hollers. Heads turn. Raskin smiles. "Once every couple of weeks," he tells me, "I have to tell him to shut up."

THE FIRST PLACE Brenda and Millie ever took me to was Edna's Restaurant, where the minister tried to pick them up. It's in a tough part of town. But as I would learn, Edna Stewart, the restaurant's owner, is a tough woman. Edna is sixty-six, and her curled hair has turned gray. She sports large rectangular-shaped eyeglass frames that are so old—more than twenty-five years—and so garish—gold-trimmed—that they actually look fashionable.

The restaurant is located on Madison Street, the main route through the West Side, which is a collection of pawn shops, currency exchanges, small clothing stores, storefront churches, and liquor stores (I once counted seventeen in a twelve-block stretch). Immediately following the death of Dr. Martin Luther King, Jr., this stretch of land went up in flames, and nearly four decades later it's still trying to recover. (Edna's, not surprisingly, was spared by arsonists during the riots.) The restaurant is sandwiched between the offices of a family doctor and a small pharmacy on the corner, and it stands across the street from a vacant lot that extends nearly an entire block. Down the street is Marshall High School, which has one of the best girls' basketball teams in the city (they have an astonishing record over the past twenty-five years of 766 games won and 84 lost, which makes it worthwhile to attend one of their games). A few blocks beyond that is Providence–St. Mel, an inner-city college prep school founded by a no-nonsense, former guidance counselor Paul Adams, who saved the school after the Archdiocese closed it in 1978, virtually abandoning the West Side.

My first visit to Edna's was on a hot summer day in 1991, and accompanying Brenda, Millie, and me was a playwright from New York who had been assigned to write the television script based on my book *There Are No Children Here.* He was a gentle, softspoken man, but after we had spent a few days together I began to get uneasy; I began to think that he didn't believe all that I'd written. So I took him to the most decrepit of the high-rises, introduced him to the meanest of the gang members, pointed out the wealthiest of the drug dealers. And on this, his last day, I thought I'd introduce him to Brenda and Millie who, I'd hoped, would affirm all that I'd written. At first, however, the lunch didn't go exactly as I'd anticipated—because Brenda and Millie, while they're realists, are also almost inexplicably upbeat. I say inexplicably, because given where they're from and what they do, they have every reason to be cynical, if not outright pessimistic. So over our lunch of fried chicken and liver, collard greens, and candied yams, Brenda and Millie filled the screenwriter not with horror stories but with tales of people who were managing, who were getting by despite all that bore down on them. Then, just as they were regaling him with inspirational tales, a young boy maybe fourteen or fifteen years old ran into the restaurant and ducked behind the heating grille. A gaggle of boys suddenly appeared outside, and one of them pulled a pistol out of a brown paper bag and started shooting. Needless to say, we feared for our lives, and we ducked under the table. As we lay there, one on top of the other, all I could think was, *Now the screenwriter will believe me.*

Then, we heard an enraged voice shouting, "What do you think you're doing? Shoo. Get away from here."

Shoo? I peered out, and there was Edna in her apron, her arms flapping, heading straight at the boy with the pistol. He didn't run, or shout, or strike back: He was too stupefied. As Edna started lecturing him, the gun dropped to his side, and while I couldn't hear what she was saying, it was clear that the shooter and his friends were hearing every word. She threw her hands up and reentered the restaurant, muttering something about "these kids should know better." As for the boys, they skulked away.

I know this is probably not the best way to lure people to Edna's. But, trust me, such an incident has never happened there since. Everyone knows Edna. "I've been here so long, my name rocks," she said, by which she means people respect her. It's the African-American equivalent of Manny's, having fed such visiting luminaries as Dick Gregory and Al Sharpton, and musicians like Flava Flav and R. Kelly. The local congressman, Danny Davis, used

Edna's to announce his reelection campaign. And Jimmy Carter lunched here when he was helping construct a nearby Habitat for Humanity home. It's also a lunch spot for local police officers.

Edna grew up on the city's South Side, and her home was a gathering place for neighborhood children, especially when they were hungry; her father, a former sharecropper, believed in a simple equation: "If someone came by, they got to eat." And so Edna and her sisters' friends ate sweet potato pie, or fried chicken, or her mother's specialty, rainbow cake. If friends stopped by on Sunday mornings, they could share in her father's pork brains and eggs, a dish that Edna serves at her restaurant.

Edna got pregnant in her sophomore year, and never finished school. She soon married, not her son's father, and they lasted eight years together. And though it's been more than forty years, her ex-husband still comes by the restaurant regularly. "He brings a container and wants his dumplings," Edna says. "He doesn't think he needs to pay. He must think we're still married."

With seven hundred dollars from her father, Edna bought the restaurant in 1966, and soon after, a mixed-race couple began frequenting the place. "They'd just come into the restaurant, sit for an hour, maybe have some cornbread and syrup," Edna recalls. "One day they said, 'Would you like some customers?' And I'm looking at 'em like, how you gonna bring me some customers?" Turns out, they were part of the advance team for Martin Luther

King, Jr., who was about to come to the city, purchase a home on the West Side, and run a campaign for open housing (which is what ultimately led to my father-in-law getting involved in testing). Edna's became the gathering spot for the civil rights workers, including Jesse Jackson and Dr. King, and she would often stay open late so they would have a place to eat after their marches.

Edna's has become a destination for European tourists looking for authentic soul food. And now business is hopping on Sundays with white folks who visit the nearby Garfield Park Conservatory, one of the nation's botanical treasures: four and a half acres of flowers and plants under one roof. The cornbread and peach cobbler are Edna's own recipes, and her favorite dish is the fried catfish. But it's her macaroni and cheese, the simplest of dishes, that may be her most popular. "No cream," she tells me. "But I'm not going to give you my recipe."

Edna doesn't know how much longer she'll keep her restaurant open. She had inquired about the vacant property across the street, and learned that the owner was asking six hundred fifty thousand, an indication that speculators have begun looking this far west. Edna told me that not long ago, on a Saturday afternoon, Wallace Davis, who owns a catfish joint down the street, called her and asked her to come down to his place.

"I'm too busy," Edna told him.

"You got to see this," Davis said.

"Maybe later," Edna replied.

"No, now. I tell you, you got to see this," Davis insisted.

So Edna took off her apron and walked the two blocks to Wallace's Catfish Corner (where on summer weekend nights, blues musicians give concerts in the adjacent parking lot). Davis took her back outside and pointed across the street. Edna saw an elderly white woman and her grown daughter tending a garden outside a brownstone. It was clear they'd just moved in.

"They're coming," Davis said.

One day, Brenda suggested we try a new place she'd discovered, so I picked her and Millie up at work, and we drove three miles west of Edna's, on Madison Street, past the blue mosquito-zapper-like lights posted high on the lampposts (they're police-run video cameras, installed to deter street crime), past the grocery store Moo and Oink, past the New World Hatter hat store, to Mac Arthur's, which may well be the West Side's most popular restaurant. On Sundays, Mac Arthur's, which serves its soul food cafeteria style, periodically has to lock its doors because the line has doubled back on itself twice. Weekdays, the wait is more reasonable, usually fifteen minutes at most. Brenda and Millie so like the food here—especially the short ribs and banana pudding—that they'll sometimes come as often as three times during the week. Besides, they tell me, they like to support Mac Arthur's because the owner has what Brenda describes as "a soft heart."

Mac Arthur Alexander, the restaurant's owner, knows nothing about food. His niece, Sharon McKennie, who manages the store and is in charge of the cooking, says, "He wouldn't know wheat bread from white bread." When I ask Alexander his favorite dish, he tells me that it's the liver, which "they deep-fry and then bake a little, or something like that." Alexander, who is fifty-eight, went to Vietnam in 1968 and returned eight months later without his left leg below the knee, the result of a mortar round that he believes was friendly fire. He now wears a prosthesis, and though he has a limp, most people don't notice. After coming home, he opened a record store, Mac's, even though he didn't know much or care much about music; then he began investing in real estate in Austin, my father-in-law's old neighborhood. He did well for himself, and decided he wanted to give back to his community. And so in 1997, he opened Mac Arthur's—in part because there wasn't a decent restaurant around, and in part because he could hire people from the neighborhood. He now employs sixty-two people. Word has since gotten out on the West Side: Mac Arthur Alexander believes there are second acts in life. "Mac," says one employee, "aims at the people who've had it hard. That's where he gets his joy. He'll give 'em nine or ten chances."

Alexander is reserved, almost shy. He arrives at work each morning, usually in a flannel shirt, and then disappears by the time lunch hour rolls around. Too many people want to talk with him, he says, often about work.

Periodically, Alexander gets letters from people in prison, asking him for a job when they get out. Alexander usually obliges, although he knows many of them won't make it. The turnover, he concedes, is high. But that seems okay with him. There's a Zen-like quality about Alexander, and when he tells me the story of how a number of years back one of his employees stole three thousand dollars from him, he seems more bemused than agitated, even though he says he has a good idea who did it. (He couldn't prove it, so he never confronted the employee; he simply had fewer people handle the restaurant's money.) "I've gotten had several times," he tells me. "But it's hard for me to fire someone. They usually fire themselves." People don't like to disappoint Alexander, so more often than not those who have done so just stop showing up for work.

One morning, I stopped by the restaurant but Alexander wasn't there. I ended up having coffee with the kitchen manager, Lewis Mosby, whom everyone calls "Cornbread." Mosby is thickly built from his years lifting weights in prison. He told me that he was fifteen when he first met Alexander; he'd hang around the record shop. Alexander took a liking to him, but Mosby subsequently got in and out of trouble so many times that he grows increasingly soft-spoken and reticent with the telling of his story. As a teenager, he was adept at hot-wiring cars, and he became the in-house car thief for the Disciples, a street gang. He'd acquire an auto—using only a screwdriver—when the gang had to move drugs or guns. Mosby soon got caught, and he served three years for car theft and possession of a gun. He was released, then got arrested again, for possession of a gun, and did another five years. He was released, and then he was involved in a gang shootout, in which a girl was accidentally injured in the crossfire. Mosby, who was arrested for the shooting, had thirteen hundred dollars on him that he couldn't explain away. He had his attorney call Alexander as a witness, hoping that Alexander would testify that he worked for him at the record shop. But when Alexander took the stand, he refused to lie; he testified that he knew Mosby was a gang member, that he hung out in front of an active drug building, and that he drove a Cadillac that had a television set in the back. Mosby cursed him under his breath, and then got sentenced to twelve years for attempted murder. Suffice it to say that he was in and out of prison twice again—at this point, to hear his story, I had to lean over the table—before his mother became ill with uterine cancer in 2000. "I wanted to be there for her," he told me. And, besides, he added, his voice now almost a whisper, "I was tired." He was forty-three years old. So, he turned to the only person he knew to turn to, Alexander. Alexander agreed to give him a job, but told him, "You're not going to make it."

Alexander believes in redemption. But he also exhibits the pragmatism of a businessman and recognizes that if his restaurant is to survive, the community around it must thrive. If his employees return to school, he'll buy their books. "You're not going to make it by working here," he

tells them. There's Maurice Gaiter, a recovering heroin ad-
dict, who now helps manage the place. And remember the
pimp Don Juan? In 1988, he discovered God and changed
his name to Bishop Don Magic Juan. For two years,
Alexander rented out a spare storefront to him for his
church and provided him with an inexpensive apartment.

Alexander, who has never raised the price of lunch
(meat and two sides for $5.95), may not know much about
food, but his recipes, which come from his sister, keep
folks coming back. (The crowd pleasers are the fried
chicken and pork chops smothered in gravy, though I tilt
toward the baked chicken with collard greens and yams on
the side.) The customers here, who have included Snoop
Dogg, the Cubs' manager Dusty Baker, and Police Superintendent Terry Hillard, are mostly blue collar, usually
lively, and mostly African-American, though not without
a sprinkling of whites and Hispanics. I, for one, eat at Mac
Arthur's more regularly than anywhere else in the city.

I caught up with Alexander a few weeks after I met
Mosby, and told him that Mosby took great pride in the
fact that he was the employee whom Alexander entrusted
with handling the restaurant's cash—at times as much as
two thousand dollars. "He trusts me," Mosby had told me.
"I can't let him down."

Alexander twirled a toothpick in his mouth. He smiled.
"I still tell him he's not going to make it," he said. "I don't
tell him he's the best I got. I don't want it going to his head.
I don't want him to know I was wrong from the beginning."

—◦◦◦—

BRENDA CALLS ME. Can I meet her at Mac Arthur's? Millie has hit a rough spot, and Brenda wants some advice, some help really, in reaching out to her friend. Mac Arthur's just seems like the natural place to consider good deeds. When I suggest to Brenda that Alexander's "soft heart" seems to wear off on others, she tells me about a previous lunch visit to Mac Arthur's. She was ordering her food when she recognized one of the servers. It was a former client of hers. Brenda didn't remember much about the woman's situation except that the last few times she'd seen her there had been a remarkable decline in her bearing. She'd appeared tired; her clothes were soiled and her hair unkempt. Brenda soon learned that she was "on the pipe," addicted to crack cocaine, and that she was shoplifting to support her habit. Brenda's worked with so many young mothers that she couldn't remember the woman's name. "Hey, girl," Brenda said when she saw the woman at Mac Arthur's. "You look good." She didn't want to say much more as she didn't want to embarrass her in front of all the customers. "I was real proud," Brenda tells me. The woman—whom Brenda thinks she might have helped get into rehab but again can't remember—smiled back, and handed Brenda her dessert, a banana pudding. "It's on me," the woman said. Brenda laughs to herself. "Ohhh," she says. "That felt good." We make a date for lunch.

Give Them What They Want

MILTON REED IS A LANKY, LONG-LEGGED MAN, and so I need to walk briskly to keep up with him. He carries a large sketch pad under one arm, and he has stashed his sketch pencils in the pockets of his beige cargo pants, along with a box opener, which he uses as a sharpener—and which also affords him some protection. He is not slowed down by his footwear: Nike running shoes from which he's cut away the heels. They resemble slippers more than sneakers. "Bought 'em too small," he explains.

We're scooting past weed-choked vacant lots and aging wood-framed homes that lean in the wind like prairie grass. We pass a group of young African-American men, one of whom halfheartedly attempts to conceal the marijuana blunt they're sharing. They turn away from us. Reed, who is also African-American, says to me, "You don't have to worry out here. They look at you, and think one thing:

There goes a cop." He lets go with his signature laugh—an uninhibited cackle that comes in small, staccato bursts, and often in response to his own observations. This is less a sign of immodesty than an acknowledgment that it's okay to laugh at his stories and perceptions, some of which can be discomfiting in their bluntness. The young men, who up to this point have been trying to deflect our notice, now turn to see what's so funny.

Reed had invited me to join him at the Bud Billiken Day Parade. Each summer, this parade winds its way through the heart of Chicago's South Side, a ribbon of predominately black neighborhoods, which runs from the Loop to Ed Sadlowski's South Chicago. (Blacks and whites still live very separate lives here, as evidenced by the El platform in the Loop at the end of the business day: Those waiting for the northbound trains are virtually all white, those on the platform awaiting the southbound trains virtually all black.) Billiken, as far as I can make out, is the country's largest parade. It lasts six hours and has fifty thousand participants. (By comparison, New York's Thanksgiving Day Parade lasts three hours and has roughly five thousand participants.) Another million people line Martin Luther King, Jr., Boulevard, ten to twenty deep in places, and some spend the night in sleeping bags to secure a good viewing spot. Virtually everyone who attends the parade is African-American. In fact, an out-of-towner stumbling upon this hopping celebration might think that it was one of black Chicago's best-kept secrets, except that it's televised on two local stations. The truth is that the city's imaginary borders can be as impenetrable as the Berlin Wall had been. A visiting friend once arrived at O'Hare airport and received a city map from a rental car agency; the map didn't include the South Side.

The parade, which is held the second Saturday in August, originated in 1928 as a salute by the *Chicago Defender* to its paperboys. The *Defender* is one of the country's oldest African-American newspapers, and though it's lost much of its vigor, in the 1930s and 1940s it was considered essential reading in the black community. Pullman porters would distribute the paper in southern towns, where it helped lure victims of segregation northward. The parade's name derived from a small statue—a "Billiken"—which sat on the editor's desk and which parade organizers claim was a Chinese god who watched over children. But Billiken, it turns out, was neither a deity nor Chinese. Around 1910, a small Chicago firm, the Billiken company, produced small figurines—sometimes in the form of penny banks—of a bullet-headed creature with pixie ears, a grinning mouth, and a rotund belly. It was the Cabbage Patch Doll of its day, a passing craze, and undoubtedly one of these figurines made its way to the desk of the *Defender*'s editor, Lucius Harper, whose nickname was "Buddy."

The parade's path winds through a part of the South Side long known as Bronzeville, a neighborhood whose ups and downs have inversely reflected the nation's mood on race. It was a thriving hub of black-owned businesses through the 1940s, the destination for blacks who fled the South in what has been hailed as one of the largest internal migrations in history. Bronzeville, where such writers as Ida B. Wells, Richard Wright, and Gwendolyn Brooks settled, was also home to Liberty Life Insurance, the first black-owned insurance company in the North, and Overton Hygienic Company, one of the foremost suppliers of African-American cosmetics. The nation's first black-commanded regiment, the 8th, was stationed at the Armory on Giles Avenue, which was named after the regiment's highest ranking officer, Lieutenant George L. Giles, who was killed in World War I. (The regiment's members held off white hoodlums during the race riots of 1919, stationing themselves on the fire escape of a nearby YMCA with their weapons.)

There's much history here. The Pilgrim Baptist Church, formerly a synagogue (in this city of ever-changing neighborhoods, churches adorned with stars of David are a common sight), was designed by Dankmar Adler, whose father was the synagogue's rabbi, and Louis Sullivan, with a helping hand from a young Frank Lloyd Wright (who worked for Adler and Sullivan's firm at the time). Some consider it one of the most beautiful Sullivan interiors. The peaked-ceiling structure boasts exquisite ornamentation, organic forms juxtaposed with geometric designs. It's also here at this church where the blues musician Thomas Dorsey pioneered modern-day black gospel music. (Dorsey authored "Precious Lord," which has been recorded by a divergent cast, from Elvis Presley to Johnny Cash.) A mile south was the old Chess Records' storefront where the Chess Brothers, Leonard and Phil, played a Little Walter recording, "Juke," and conducted an early version of test marketing, placing a speaker in the corner doorway to see if people at the adjacent bus stop responded. And there's Meyers Ace Hardware, once the site of the Sunset Café (which later became the Grand Terrace), a hotbed of jazz in the 1920s and 1930s. Earl Hines and Cab Calloway performed here regularly as did Louis Armstrong, who titled one song "Sunset Stop." Musicians still come by the hardware store often, since, as one once said, "This place is as sacred to jazz musicians as the Wailing Wall is to Jews." The store's owner was once offered ten thousand dollars for a mural in one of the back offices, past the screwdrivers and furnace filters; it depicts a trio of musicians and a sultry singer whose head is cut off by wood paneling. Another time, twelve German trumpet players came here; each purchased plungers, and had the store's owner sign them.

In the 1960s, when white establishments opened their doors to blacks, many of the businesses in Bronzeville suffered, and most eventually went under. The community is undergoing a revival, in large part because of a thriving black middle class committed to staying in the city and rebuilding this historic neighborhood.

Milton Reed has come to the parade in the hope of earning some money by drawing profiles. The previous summer, he told me, he made more than three hundred dollars, charging seven dollars a portrait. A line had formed in the morning, and it never let up. Reed and I reach the corner of King Drive and Muddy Waters Drive (the city has so many honorary streets, many named after obscure personages like Daniel D. "Moose" Brindisi and the Reverend Frenchie Smith, that it's lost count), and Reed has me purchase two milk crates at a dollar apiece, so he can have a place for him and his subjects to sit while he sketches. "Let me get to work," he announces, although there doesn't seem to be much work to be had. No one has approached him. I use one of the crates as a platform so that I can see the parade over the crowd. From a nearby vendor, Reed orders himself a small container of rib tips, then worries it might get his hands too messy, so instead asks for a Polish sausage. I holler for him to get me some of the jerk chicken. The food is plentiful, as are renegade vendors whom the city, on this occasion, traditionally chooses to ignore.

I FIRST MET Reed in 1999, while visiting a woman in the Stateway Gardens Public Housing complex, which was then a collection of eight seventeen-story high-rises. He was in the living room of my hostess, where he was painting a gold-trimmed black panther on the cinderblock wall. He had a forty-ounce bottle of Colt 45 beside him, and he was so completely engaged in his work that he didn't say a word. There was nothing out of the ordinary about the rendering, though it was clear that Reed had taken great care with it. He had first sketched the outlines of the panther in pencil, using a ruler and right angle, and then had gone to work with oil-based house paint. Because of its permanence, there was little room for error. I assumed at the time that the panther was meant to conjure up more radical days. I later learned, however, that a number of years before a woman had asked Reed to paint a black panther with gold trim on her kitchen wall to match her black and gold furniture, a common color pairing among public-housing residents. ("They all follow that same tradition," Reed told me.) Word quickly spread, and soon Reed had a reputation. Public-housing residents came to know him as "Mr. Artist"—as in "Mr. Artist, how much you charge for one of them murals?"

Reed, who's now in his late forties, has salt-and-pepper hair and a trimmed beard and mustache. He likes to talk, and he unabashedly offers his opinions to just about anyone, including to the cadre of young drug dealers outside his building. "They tell me they're in business," he says. "I tell 'em they need to get a real job." Reed's full-time job is as a maintenance worker at the Dearborn Homes, the public-housing complex where he lives. Since the early 1990s, however, Reed has been kind of a Diego Rivera of the projects, painting the imaginings and realities of the dispossessed, of the men and women who live in America's poorest neighborhood, an area beset with the kinds of problems one might expect in a place where ninety percent of the families are headed by a single parent and where violence has become such a way of life that a banner on a local church calls for a "Peace Truce" and a local tombstone maker, Elmo's, advertises, "While U Wait. Before You Go, See Elmo."

Reed himself grew up in public housing, in the Robert Taylor Homes, a complex of twenty-eight buildings adjacent to Stateway. The Robert Taylor Homes and Stateway Gardens stretched over two miles, the longest contiguous alignment of public housing in the world. Reed liked to draw as a kid, and after dropping out of high school, he earned his GED and went on to a junior college, where he took commercial art classes. He then worked for eight years at a graphic arts firm, and while he didn't particularly like the job—it stifled his creativity, he says—the company did send him to more art classes, where he learned about perspective and composition.

He began his part-time career as a professional artist by painting fairly mundane likenesses: apples, oranges, and peaches in people's kitchens; cartoon characters like Betty Boop, the Flintstones, and Pikachu on the walls of children's rooms; fish and dolphins in bathrooms. Also, early on, he was often asked to sketch likenesses of Jesus Christ, but it irked him that virtually everyone wanted Jesus to be white. It was as if people had been beaten down for so long that they no longer believed that anyone who resembled themselves could amount to much. "They'll say, 'Why you draw him so dark?' " he told me. "I'll say, 'Jesus wasn't really white,' and they'll say, 'Look, I'm paying you, do it the way I say. I know how Jesus look.' I mean, they probably met Jesus in person, so I can't argue with them. I give 'em what they want."

Soon, people began to make personalized requests. First, there were the panthers. Then, of all things, it was landscapes. He remembers the first time it happened. A young woman told Reed she wanted a sky with clouds over water and trees. She said she wanted the sunlight coming off the water. "I said, 'I understand,' " Reed recalls. " 'Let me try to make you feel good.' " The landscapes caught on. Drab cinderblock walls became lakes surrounded by oak trees. Beaches with palm trees. People so treasured these soothing natural scenes that they'd throw parties where friends could get their pictures taken in front of them. It was as close as many of them would get to finding a refuge from the dankness of their neighborhood.

Women asked Reed to paint them lounging by the water, a vicarious escape. Soon, one asked Reed to paint her by her lake naked, and that, too, caught on. Reed, though, refused to have women model in the buff out of fear that their boyfriends might not approve, and so he'd undress them in his head. One client told Reed, "Oooh, that look just like me. That's how my breasts look. It's just like you was looking at me. You got a good imagination."

Disapproval in this neighborhood can get ugly, and Reed quickly discovered that people didn't take kindly if he painted the same mural in one apartment that he'd done in another. Reed told me that once, in an elevator, a client threatened to beat him up if he didn't change a neighbor's landscape, and so now he always makes sure to choose different hues for the water, or rearrange the placement of the trees, or choose different kinds of trees. "I'm giving them something," he told me, "that they can never have in their life unless they was rich." And so, he goes on to say, they want something that reflects their own sensibilities. They want something unique because there's not much they can call their own.

Reed keeps a record of all his murals, but he never signs his work, out of fear that the housing authority might come after him for defacing their property, though truthfully they should have been compensating him for beautification—and, on occasion, for keeping people out of trouble. Once, a woman who lived on the tenth floor asked Reed to paint the city's downtown skyline on her living room wall so that it would be as if you were looking right through the cinderblock at the John Hancock Building and Sears Tower lit up at night. Reed charged her one hundred fifty dollars. "It's just like you were looking right outside," he said. He came back the following week to put some finishing touches on the mural, and the woman asked him for one other thing, to draw a rendering of her, off to the side, with one arm pushing forward, as if she were reaching for the clouds. "It looked as if she was dancing," he said. Then she made one final request, that he draw her boyfriend, away from her, upside down. "Make sure you put his face in there, so I know it's him," she told Reed. So, he drew him upside down just as she'd asked, his feet straight up in the air. When he stepped back, he realized that he'd drawn this woman pushing her boyfriend out the window. "Instead of murdering that guy," Reed said laughing, "she can take her fantasy out like that."

Not all of it makes sense to him. "I hate to tell you," he said. "Some people got some weird imaginations." One woman asked him to paint on one wall a rendering of Jesus (Caucasian, of course), and on another wall a man, standing, his pants unzipped, urinating on a tree. "I can't know what goes on in these people's heads," he said. "I would think that that's wrong, just to have a person on the wall, taking a leak. And then she said, 'I don't like that penis, make it bigger.' So I says, 'Wanda, they don't come that size.' She says, 'Maybe yours don't.' So I did it. Just like she asked."

Some of Reed's work reflects the fact that death is very much a part of this neighborhood. Drug dealers, with their deep pockets, are his modern-day Medicis. One asked Reed to paint scenes of a young man injuring a policeman, an officer getting shot as he exited his squad car, and an officer getting run over. He obliges such requests because the money can be quite good, and they treat him to free beers, but he despises the work. He can only hope that maybe his renderings will be cathartic and thus help forestall future confrontations between the drug dealers and the police. (Once, he heard that the police were looking for the artist who had done these murals, and he made sure to disappear for a while.) More often, though, his customers request tombstones that read REST IN PEACE and include the name of the deceased friend or relative. In one apartment, a gentleman asked him to draw ten of them in his bedroom. "You know what?" Reed says. "I think it really helped a lot of people, kind of calmed them down."

REED'S NOW STANDING on his milk crate as well. He seems to have forgotten his reason for being here, and offers a running commentary on the parade. The city's mayor, Richard M. Daley, passes by in a convertible, looking unusually relaxed. No mayor has ever missed this parade. In fact, it's drawn such political luminaries as Harry Truman and Adlai Stevenson, as well as figures like Muhammad Ali and Nat "King" Cole. Reed's shaking his head. "I want to ask the mayor, 'Why'd you do that to Meigs Field the way you did?' Now you know that wasn't right." The demolition of the single runway at Meigs Field, an airport for private planes, was an old-school move by a new-school politician. Earlier in the summer, under cover of night, the mayor had sent a battalion of backhoes and bulldozers to scar the runway with gigantic X-shaped trenches, rendering useless this small lakefront airport—which he wants to rebuild as a park. King Richard the Second, Chicagoans joked—a reference, of course, to King Richard the First, his father. (Between the two of them, they've governed

Chicago for thirty-five of the last fifty years.) The thing about it, I argue with Reed, is that the mayor was probably right: This prime piece of lakefront property belongs to the people, not to the few who can afford their own airplanes. "Yeah, but it ain't the right way to go 'bout things," he argues.

Of a smiling alderman who is followed by fifty supporters wearing T-shirts bearing his name, Reed remarks, "They should be throwing milk cartons at him." When the fifty-four-year-old county treasurer, Maria Pappas, jumps out of a convertible to spiritedly twirl a baton, Reed laughs good-heartedly, and applauds out of admiration. A number of white politicians drive by, each accompanied by a black friend or coworker; it seems like a statement—"I have friends who are black"—from another era. But it's the high-stepping, boogying marching bands that get the crowd worked up, especially the South Shore Drill Team, which stops every couple of blocks to perform their highly choreographed and high-spirited routine.

The Jesse White Tumblers march by; they're a group of kids from Cabrini Green, another public-housing complex, who can be seen at events throughout the city, including at halftime during Chicago Bulls games. "Oh, shit," exclaims Reed. "There's gonna be some jumping now." A woman eager to see the tumblers gives me a flirtatious look and climbs onto my milk crate alongside me, her buxom body pressed against mine. A young man hawking bottles of water and sporting a tattoo on his forearm of his deceased pit bull (which, he later tells me, was named "Cats") winks at my good fortune.

Reed climbs down and tells me he's got to get to work. But there are no takers, so he instructs me to sit down and begins to sketch me. Passersby stop to peek over his shoulder; he points to my eyes and eyeglasses and observes, "All this should be smaller, but it's a nice drawing of a white guy." A teenage girl takes a look and reprimands Reed. "His glasses ain't square," she tells him. He erases the glasses and makes them circular.

A mother comes by with her five-year-old daughter, sits her on my milk crate, and asks—really, tells—Reed to draw her. The child sits surprisingly still, a bag of blue cotton candy in her lap, and then it starts to rain, so the mother and I hold a sheet of plastic over Reed's head as the girl pushes the cotton candy under her leg to keep it dry. "What d'ya think?" he says, holding the sketch up for the mother to see. She examines the sketch, which is marked by raindrops. "Where her buttons?" she asks. Reed looks perplexed. "On her shirt," she says, pointing to her daughter. Reed looks over. He's missed the shirt's buttons, so he draws them in, and because of the rain he charges the mother five dollars instead of the usual seven.

"I'm ready to get outta here," Reed tells me after a couple of hours. Business is slow. We walk north on King Drive, stopping occasionally to watch a high school marching band, then the Broken Arrow Riding Club (a collection of African-American horsemen and -women), then a flatbed truck bearing Jesse Jackson and members of his Operation PUSH, and finally a float of black owners of McDonald's franchises.

WE HEAD WEST on 45th Street, toward what used to be the Robert Taylor Homes, the complex where Reed grew up. It is now a vast tract of open land. Reed refers to it simply as "what was."

This is a city in motion, a place of passages. Chicago's public-housing high-rises have long stood as cinderblock monuments to our disregard—some might say outright hostility—toward the poor. When the bulk of the high-rises were built, in the 1950s and 1960s, white aldermen didn't want them in their neighborhoods, and so they were placed at the edge of already existing ghettos; because real estate was in short supply, they reached upward to the heavens. As a result, public housing served as a bulwark to segregation: For decades, these buildings have symbolized America's disdain for its less fortunate.

But there's been a remarkable turn of events in the city that Nelson Algren once described as so audacious that it dared to "roll boulevards down out of pig-wallows and roll its dark river uphill." If promises are kept and plans met, all of Chicago's eighty-two public-housing family high-rises will be gone by 2010, having fallen to the wrecking ball. Erase the slate and start anew. It's the equivalent of tearing down a city with the population of Des Moines; at its peak in the early 1990s, the Chicago Housing Authority housed two hundred thousand people. Plans are in place to build new homes in their stead, some of which will be allotted for those displaced, others selling, at least in one gentrifying community, for upwards of four hundred thousand dollars. This redevelopment strategy is presented as a grand gesture to right past wrongs: to build mixed-income communities, to integrate, if not by race, at least by class.

It's also a classic instance of Chicago's daring and incautious nature. On the one hand, these mixed-income communities may well be like phoenixes rising from the ashes, a far more palatable alternative to the ghettos they have replaced. On the other hand, it is unclear what will happen to the thousands of poor families who once lived in these housing complexes, and for whom there's not room in the newly constructed homes. In 1963, when Mayor Richard J. Daley declared, "There are no ghettos in Chicago," most knew better: When you drove into the city from the south, you were faced with the two-mile-long curtain of high-rises; the squalor was impossible to ignore. Now, many of Chicago's poor families are being scattered to the winds, finding their way outward to the city's rim of equally troubled neighborhoods and to a ring of already struggling suburbs; this movement mirrors what has happened in European cities, such as Paris, where the poor, like a wreath, encircle the urban centers. For most, they will be no better off, and now completely out of sight, an urban problem that has been exported and dispensed with rather than resolved.

You might think that the demolition of the projects is bad news for Reed, but, in fact, he's busier than ever. His patrons are calling on him to replicate the landscapes, the Jesus Christs, and the tombstones in their new residences. But many are also asking for something simpler: a visual memento of the place they used to live. Despite the hellishness of these high-rises, for many they were home.

After the parade, Reed and I walk back to his apartment in a Dearborn Homes mid-rise which, unlike the surrounding high-rises, will undergo renovation rather than demolition. Reed's living room is sparsely furnished with a sofa and an easy chair, both covered in plastic sheeting. On the floor is a recently purchased carton of Newports and a case of Miller beer, as well as his television. He lifts the TV and feels underneath for some cash he's hidden there; he's going shopping for more paint and an easel. On one wall, I see three nearly identical sketches of a cluster of high-rises; each one is titled simply "Robert Taylor 1962–2000." The rendering is quite literal, like a photograph, and in fact the neighborhood looks lifeless, which seems odd given the stupefying energy of these high-rises. As I look at the sketches, I realize what's missing: people. Their absence is not unintentional. "It's like a ghost town," he explains.

Reed sells these for twenty dollars apiece, but he tells

me that many want the projects painted on the walls of their new homes. "In the front room," he tells me. "The first thing you'll see walking into their house. Can you imagine? The first thing that pops into your mind is, You must have lived in the Robert Taylor Homes or known someone." His laughter punctuates his thoughts. "And they want everybody to know this."

But Reed prefers to dwell on his efforts to expand his customers' horizons rather than re-creating the past, and so soon he's pacing back and forth again, talking once more about his fantastical murals. "Go ahead on and give these people something that they could never have in their life," he tells me. "Give it to them, and it will make them happy."

26th Street

CHICAGO'S CRIMINAL COURTS BUILDING IS A MAS-
sive columned structure made of limestone; I'm told
that it has the world's largest collection of felony court-
rooms (thirty-four) under one roof. Roughly forty thousand cases are heard here each year, an average of 153 a
day. The rush of humanity is staggering. The central bond
court, room 101, begins proceedings at one o'clock every
afternoon, and it is so backed up with the newly arrested
that defendants now appear on video from lockup in the
basement. Court officials say that bringing all of them into
the courtroom would pose insurmountable security problems, so friends and family members, often with young
children, sit on the hard-backed benches and watch their
loved ones appear on televisions hanging from the ceiling.
The judge goes through the defendant's past record, then
sets a bond. It usually takes a minute, maybe two. One at-

torney commented, "You can't help but be overwhelmed by the speed with which things happen here."

But for some the wheels of justice turn a little more quickly than for others. Carved into the building's stone exterior is a single word, VERITAS, and indeed while the truth more often than not eventually comes to light, it is not necessarily pursued with equal vigor in every case. Consider the tale of Police Commander Jon Burge. Over the course of eighteen years, ninety defendants—all of whom had been interrogated by Burge or by a small group of detectives under his command—appeared in various courtrooms here, accused of crimes like arson and murder. Over time, each claimed he had been tortured. Some said they'd been suffocated, a plastic bag or typewriter cover held over their heads until they passed out. Some claimed they'd been given electric shocks, administered by a cattle prod or a field-telephone-like device, their genitals the usual target. Still others said that Burge and his men had played sadistic games with them, placing guns in their mouths. But it took seventeen years before anyone paid attention to these claims, and then only after a dogged local journalist, John Conroy, wouldn't let the story go. Burge, who has since been dismissed from the police force, is now—twenty-nine years after the first claim—under investigation; a special prosecutor has been appointed to see whether there are grounds to prosecute Burge or any of the officers under his command. Many of those who say they were tortured by Burge and his men remain in prison, though in January 2003 Governor Ryan pardoned and released four of the convicted who were on death row, arguing they were innocent of the crimes to which they'd allegedly given confessions. The goings-on in this building, like my father-in-law's sculpture of the anvil hanging precariously over the birdfeeder, represent the ultimate juxtaposition of power and fragility.

The building is known among its regulars as "26th Street," a nod to its location at the corner of 26th Street and California Avenue, which is seven miles southwest of the Loop, the city's hub—a rather long distance, given the import of what occurs here. It is, as one lawyer told me, "an island unto itself." Many people assume that the building was intentionally placed far from the center of things to keep the riffraff away from downtown, but in reality, it's the result, ironically enough, of questionable dealings. This strip of land was once owned by Anton Cermak, a Bohemian immigrant who was elected mayor in 1931, and while Cermak was president of the Cook County Board, he sold the land to the county, presumably for a profit. (Cermak was assassinated in 1933 while standing next to President Franklin Roosevelt at a political rally in Miami, Florida. It's fairly well accepted that the lone assassin had meant to kill the president, but many Chicagoans believed—and still do—that Al Capone's successors had ordered Cermak's murder because he intended to crack down on the mob so that he might assert his own control over their illicit operations.)

When someone new moves to Chicago, one of the first places I steer them to is 26th Street. It may well be the most consequential building in the city. It is certainly the liveliest. A lawyer once told me that he found working there addictive—that although he would periodically try cases in the more rarefied atmosphere of the civil courts, he always found his way back. There have been times I've gone to 26th Street for a particular trial and ended up spending the day there, wandering from courtroom to courtroom and eavesdropping on conversations in the hallways, like the one a woman was having with her friend on a cell phone. "He got himself a good lawyer," she told her friend. "He got himself a Jew lawyer. The man is mad."

ANDREA LYON IS a mad lawyer, which, as the woman on the cell phone intuited about her friend's attorney, probably explains Lyon's success as well. In nineteen capital cases, she has saved all of her clients from the electric chair. Lyon is an outsized figure: six feet tall, broad-shouldered, and sturdily built. "What does size matter?" you might reasonably ask. But in such a macho environment, trust me, it does. Lyon began practicing in this building as a public defender, in 1978, and at the time she was one of only a handful of women lawyers here; there were no women judges at all. In those early days, one judge stubbornly referred to Lyon alternately as "sir," "gentleman," and "Mr. Lyon." "At first I thought it was a slip of the tongue," Lyon recalled. "But it became quite pointed. I'd pretend I had this little tape recorder that I'd turn on in the morning and it would say, 'This is your problem, it's not my problem. This is your problem, it's not my problem.' " It calmed her down—and Lyon, by her own admission, occasionally needs calming down. One colleague recalls the time a prosecutor, during a break in the courtroom, called Lyon a vile name: Lyon responded by grabbing him by the collar and nearly lifting him off his feet. (It was this reaction, Lyon believes, that finally earned her the respect of her male colleagues.) When I mentioned Lyon's name to a judge, he smiled. "She can heat things up," he said.

Another story that has long made the rounds—and that Lyon confirmed for me—is that many years ago, when Lyon was in law school in Washington, D.C., a man tried to mug her while she was walking home late one night. But when he grabbed her by the arm and reached for her purse, Lyon responded by slugging him and knocking him to the ground, breaking his jaw. "I couldn't leave him there bleeding," she said. "So I called an ambulance. I'm such a public defender."

Lyon, who now works out of DePaul University's Law School (in the Loop), where she operates a clinic that handles primarily capital murder cases, invited me to join her one morning at 26th Street, where she had to file two rather routine motions in two separate cases. Cases are called at nine-thirty in the morning, so it's best to get there early to find parking. As you pass through the metal detectors (which have turned up knives disguised as various items, including a lipstick container, a lighter, and a house key), you may spot a jacketless gentleman in white shirt and tie chatting with passersby. He's the chief judge, Paul Biebel, who makes a point every morning to position himself at the building's entrance so that he can talk with public defenders, prosecutors, police officers, and sheriff's deputies. On this particular day, a court administrator pauses to alert Judge Biebel to the rumor that there's a man in the building practicing law without a license. The judge's brother, a defense attorney, stops to say hello. (His other siblings—three brothers and a sister—are all in law enforcement.) Two women pass by in T-shirts that have wedding pictures of Tina Ball on them. Ball was the mother of seven and a flagger at a highway construction site; she had been hit and killed by a drunk driver, Thomas Harris, who had four previous DUI convictions. These two women had been friends of Ball, and the message on the back of their T-shirts urged Harris's conviction for murder. "There's a passion in this place," says Biebel.

Two things are immediately apparent to newcomers here. All the defendants, if they're not coming directly from the jail and thus appearing in their olive-colored jail garb, are dressed in casual attire. In the summer, men appear in shorts, women in miniskirts. Usually the men arrive in T-shirts, oversized jeans, and basketball shoes. Once, a defendant accused of rape appeared in a black leather jacket with PIMPING AIN'T EASY embroidered on the back. A private investigator who spends much of his time at 26th Street told me, "They're making a statement: 'I don't respect this setting enough to pull out my best outfit.'" (The police department's tactical officers, for their part, are immediately recognizable by their dress as well: usually, shirts and jackets bearing the logos of sports teams.) The other notable quality about the defendants here is that they are overwhelmingly African-American and Hispanic. As one attorney told me, "26th Street makes it look like Chicago's an entirely minority town." Roughly eighty-eight percent of the eleven thousand awaiting trial in the neighboring county jail are black and Hispanic. There are those who argue, "Well, that's who's committing all the crimes," but given that an estimated seventy percent of the cases are for possession or selling of narcotics, the racial makeup of the defendants seems rather lopsided. Blacks or Hispanics, after all, are no more or less likely to use drugs than whites. Judge Michael Toomin, who has served twenty-three years on the bench, and who displays a copy of the Magna Carta in his courtroom (along with his high school equivalency certificate), complains that the drug cases "are nickel-and-dime stuff." What's more, he says, only forty-five slots are available in rehab programs for defendants with drug problems. "That's abysmal," he sighs.

I wait for Lyon in a third-floor courtroom where the judge has yet to arrive. Two young men lean over the back of their bench and listen intently to another man, who looks to be in his forties. His head is shaved and he has a significant paunch. He's on trial for heroin possession. "I haven't been in trouble in five years, but you can't beat the system," he lectures, his audience nodding their heads in affirmation. "They give me two years, I'll take it." ("Sometimes the prosecution is right," Lyon says, "which is why God made guilty pleas.") A woman across the aisle twirls a cigar in her fingers. "Let's smoke this blunt," she jokes. The courtroom erupts in laughter.

Lyon arrives, dressed smartly in a navy blue suit and sensible shoes. When she wants to soften her appearance, she'll wear pink or baby blue. So that her size doesn't appear intimidating, she'll kneel by the side of witnesses or joke about her height with jurors. "Nobody would think twice about a big guy," she says.

There are two kinds of courtrooms in the building: old and new. The old courts are deep, cavernous spaces in which the judge's bench is thirty feet from the first row of spectator benches. You have to lean forward and listen hard to hear the exchanges between the judge and lawyers. The newer courts are smaller, and have a floor-to-ceiling bulletproof glass wall separating the spectators from the proceedings, which are piped in by an audio system. It's like being in a glass bubble. These rooms are so small that it's difficult for lawyers to have a conversation among themselves or with their clients without being overheard by the jury. Once, in a robbery case, a frustrated defense attorney put his head down on the table during a cross-examination of a witness. "Wake up, wake up, you got to do something," his client whispered into his ear. The jury could hear every word. We're in one of these newer court-rooms, and the court clerk permits me to sit in the jury box along with three uniformed police officers waiting to testify in another case. When the judge arrives, he asks me who I am. I tell him, and assure him that his clerk had okayed my presence. "This is my courtroom," he scolds. "Not my clerk's." Later, during a break, I tell the clerk that perhaps I should go back to the judge's chambers to apologize. "Apologize?" she laughs. "He's just got his underpants on too tight this morning."

Lyon's client, Oily Thomas, has been sentenced to seventy years for shooting a rival drug dealer on the city's South Side. Thomas was identified by four witnesses, and a baseball cap similar to the one worn by Thomas was found at the scene. But two of the witnesses have re-canted, and one of them has testified that he was paid co-caine by the victim's family so that they could pin the murder on Thomas and get him off their turf. Lyon tells me she also has an eyewitness who is willing to testify that she saw the crime, and that she had told the police they had the wrong man. Lyon is trying to get Thomas a new trial; this morning, she asks for a little extra time to respond to the prosecution's opposition to dismiss the appeal, and her request is granted. Lyon's cases are procedural today, and so her usual theatrics are absent. She once handcuffed one of her wrists to a pipe along the courtroom wall to demonstrate to a jury how her client had to sit for three days while awaiting an interrogation. Another time, she placed her client in the center of the courtroom, and with masking tape measured off the size of the small room he'd been placed in by the police; then she had all five of the officers who'd been present for the interrogation enter the space. She wanted to demonstrate to the jury the intimidating nature of the setup, but her demonstration proved more effective than she had bargained for when her client started shaking involuntarily.

On the day I joined her, her other client was facing charges of shooting and killing a liquor store proprietor. It seemed like a straightforward case. Glen Jones had been accused of entering the store with two friends intending to rob it. The store owner grabbed for his pistol, which he was wearing on a holster. Shooting ensued, and as Jones fled, he allegedly fired his gun, killing the owner. It was all caught on videotape. "At first blush, it looks like there's nowhere to go, that it's a dead-bang loser," Lyon tells me. "But things aren't necessarily as they seem." Lyon, with the help of a private investigator, is working on the theory that the store owner was dealing in guns, and that Jones and his cohorts had come back to the store to return a defective weapon. An argument ensued, Lyon believes, and the store owner began shooting first. Lyon thinks she can make the case that her client acted in self-defense.

This is, indeed, a place where the world can seem topsy-turvy. Once, a man accused of double murder chose to represent himself and told the jury that he turned himself in after hearing he was wanted on the TV news. Only problem was he had also argued that he had been in custody at the time of the murder. Nonetheless, the jury acquitted him.

Of course what you see in this building is a rather small but influential corner of the city; and, it can be a very nasty corner. The street gangs, in particular, wield enormous influence. Symbols of their power—pitchforks, six-pointed stars, and crowns—are everywhere, etched into courtroom doors and courtroom benches. In 1988, when forty-one-year-old Jeff Fort, leader of the El Rukn gang, and four of his generals were tried for the murder of a rival gang member, Willie "Dollar Bill" Bibbs, the court took extraordinary security precautions, including the construction of a pillbox in the hallway where a deputy sheriff sat armed with a machine gun. They also placed snipers on the rooftop and escorted the judge home each day after court. (Fort was convicted and sentenced to seventy-five years; he was already in prison, serving an eighty-year sentence for directing a terrorist-for-hire plot on behalf of Libya.)

I ask Lyon whether, after twenty-five years of trying

cases in which someone has taken the life of another, often in a quite brutal fashion, her work hasn't tainted her view of humanity. She replies that it hasn't—that in fact she'd been buoyed by periodic displays of nobility, including the time the mother of a murdered prostitute told Lyon that she didn't want her daughter's killer put to death because, she said, "I don't want to be like him." Later in our conversation, however, Lyon tells me that if there's one lesson she's learned at 26th Street it's that "the line is thin and anyone can cross it. Anyone. I used to think 'I'm a nice, loving person. There's no way I could ever commit a violent act.' But you do this long enough, you know anyone can kill. Anyone. Under the right circumstances. If you understand that, then maybe you have a little more appreciation for the freedoms you have here. It isn't someone else's problem."

I meekly suggest to her that maybe her perception of the world *has* changed some—or, at least, that it's different from those of us who are not at 26th Street on a regular basis. She doesn't exactly deny it. Instead, she tells me the story of a friend in private practice who once told Lyon that he didn't feel like "a real lawyer" except when he was at 26th Street. "I know what he meant," she tells me. "When I walk into that building, I feel like I'm coming home. It's hard to explain exactly."

It Takes All Kinds

W HEN I FIRST MOVED TO CHICAGO IN 1983, I rented an apartment in Wicker Park, a neighborhood of modest redbrick apartment buildings and wood-framed family homes, although on Pierce Avenue there's a row of majestic Victorian houses built at the turn of the century by German merchants, the nouveaux riches of their day who were looking to make a statement that they'd made it. When I arrived, the area was in transition, an amalgam of old Germans and Poles, young Hispanic families, and young white artists. The places to hang out then were the Busy Bee, a Polish coffee shop that served pierogis and potato pancakes, and the basketball courts in the park from which the neighborhood derived its name.

I lived on a street shaped like a boomerang, just across the street from the basketball courts; even on weekday afternoons, I could usually find a game there. I was single then, and lived on the third floor of a three-flat, a narrow redbrick building that was warmed by built-in gas space heaters in the middle of each kitchen. (They're still common in the city's older buildings.) The single heater's pencil-thin flames were hardly enough to warm the four-room apartment, and by early winter a sheet of ice would form on the inside of my windows. It would get so cold come January that I'd move my mattress to the kitchen floor, next to the heater. There were three of us in the building. On the first floor was a guy who ran a bike repair shop out of his apartment, and just downstairs from me were two men in their twenties who spent their days shooting up heroin and their nights looking for ways to finance their habit—which at one point included crawling through the transom above my back door and relieving me of my rather feeble stereo system and record collection.

Soon after I arrived, I learned that Nelson Algren had lived down the block, where he had written *A Walk on the Wild Side* and carried on his transatlantic affair with Simone de Beauvoir. Two years earlier, friends of Algren (he died in 1981) had convinced the city to change the name of the street to Algren Avenue, but residents complained vigorously, not because of any distaste for Algren but because the change of address would pose too much of an inconvenience: It would mean changing their licenses and insurance policies. It was a measure of Algren's stature here (or lack of it) that the residents won, and the city returned the street to its original name, Evergreen Avenue.

Algren, I suspect, wouldn't have been terribly surprised by this turn of events. He always felt unloved by the city that served as his muse, and in his later years he moved to New York, where he hoped that he might be embraced and appreciated. (Algren's not the only well-known writer who has moved through Chicago; the city's best often leave, or simply pass through: Saul Bellow, Richard Wright, Sherwood Anderson, Ben Hecht.) While in Chicago, Algren had written of the city's underbelly, of its dispossessed, its prostitutes and junkies, its hustlers and con artists. He lived life hard; he was a drinker and a gambler. His lustful, prickly ballad to the city, *Chicago: City on the Make,* may be the best thing ever written about this city (along with Carl Sandburg's collection, *Chicago Poems*), yet it didn't find an audience here until Jean-Paul Sartre translated it into French, and it won overseas acclaim. And while he writes in the poem that "You can't belong to Chicago," he clearly loved this place. Listen to him on riding the El:

> *By nights when the yellow salamanders of the El bend*
> *all one way and the cold rain runs with the red-lit rain.*
> *By the way the city's million wires are burdened only by*
> *lightest snow; and the old year yet lighter upon them.*
> *When chairs are stacked and glasses are turned and*
> *arc-lamps all are dimmed.*
> *By days when the wind bangs alley gates ajar and*
> *the sun goes by on the wind.*

Never a City So Real

By nights when the moon is an only child above
the measured thunder of
the cars, you may know Chicago's heart at last.

There is a monument to Algren. It's an unremarkable fountain, eighteen feet in diameter, set in a small triangular park where three major thoroughfares meet: Ashland Avenue, Milwaukee Avenue, and Division Street. It is an intersection of the new and the old, of the rich and the poor, of the lively and the lifeless, of the artists and the artful. The park is a refuge for drifters and day laborers, the very slice of the city Algren wrote about, and, indeed, engraved at the foot of the fountain is a quote from *City on the Make*: "For the masses who do the city's labor also keep the city's heart." But the neighborhood is changing, and in the mornings young men in gray suits and young women in white blouses and somber skirts merge here to catch the bus or the El downtown. The Busy Bee, once the anchor here, is gone, replaced by restaurants that require reservations and bars so well lit you could read a newspaper in them. Families have razed old homes and built anew. After all, neighborhoods in Chicago change direction regularly; in another part of town, for instance, you have Mexican-Americans occupying Pilsen, which was originally a community of Czechs and was named after Plzeň, the second largest city in Czechoslovakia. But in Wicker Park it's unclear who the insiders are and who the outsiders are, and so you have Spring, one of the city's posher, trendier restaurants, at one corner of the neighborhood, and Polska Restauracja Podhalanka, which has been around for twenty years, at another. It's as if the neighborhood is simultaneously moving both backward and forward in time.

ROBERT GUINAN IS an artist whose inspiration, like Algren's, comes from the street, from the people who are seen but not heard, and for that reason I had wanted to meet him. He suggested that we rendezvous just a block west of Triangle Park at Rite Liquors on Division Street, the bar where he had spent many years drinking and sketching. This is Algren's old turf. I waited beneath the tavern's tired-looking green awning, watching its collection of neon signs—BUDWEISER, GO BEARS, a green shamrock, DRINK STRAIGHT FROM THE BOTTLE—toss flickers of light on the cracked sidewalk. A thick-legged elderly woman entered Rite Liquors, and I could hear a voice from inside announce good-naturedly, "Here comes that dancing gigolo." "What?" the woman growled. "What y'a say?" The man and his friend chuckled. Then a man who was missing a good number of teeth and wearing a T-shirt that read LICK IT SLAM IT SUCK IT came up and offered to sell me a sledgehammer. It was wrapped in electrical tape and looked as worn as he did. When I declined, he flung the mallet over his shoulder and tried the other customers in the bar, who turned down his offer as well.

Rite Liquors is like a spinster among the young and the beautiful. Directly across the street are two new stores: Smack, a clothing boutique, and Bamboo Nail Spa. There's a Starbucks on the corner, and down the street a sushi bar and the Smoke Daddy, a rib joint (which despite the fact that it is relatively trendy has some of the best ribs in the city, along with live blues bands). But Rite Liquors refuses to give ground. Patrons, mostly men, still beat the bar's owner to work, waiting under the awning at seven a.m. for the doors to open and for the beer and whiskey to flow.

"It's still here." The voice has a warbly quality to it. Guinan, who at sixty-nine is slightly built and light-footed, has sneaked up behind me. His face, which looks alternately dour, amused, and baffled, is almost cartoonish-looking in its pliability; Guinan has the expressiveness of a mime. Guinan was once a regular at Rite Liquors, where he would come to sketch two patrons in particular. One was a young blonde bartender, Dorota, who had come from Poland just a few years earlier, and who complained to Guinan that his sketches made her appear unhappy. (The bartenders at Rite Liquors still tend to be recently ar-rived young Polish women.) The other was Loretta, an African-American woman who had worked in a commer-cial printing facility for years until her hands mysteriously broke out in a bad case of eczema. She was on disability when Guinan met her, drinking to fill the void in her life. Embarrassed by the unsightliness of her hands, she wore black leather gloves, which made her look exotic among the young men in torn leather jackets and the old-timers in frayed shirts.

Guinan hadn't been here for a number of years, but little has changed; the place is still owned by Michael Liacopoulos, who came over from southern Greece and purchased it from a Jewish man in 1982. As you walk in, there's a liquor store to the left, and to the right, running the length of the seventy-foot store, is a narrow, handsome bar made of oak. A thirty-five-year-old Budweiser clock hangs over its center; a nineteen-inch television sits at one end. A pool table is in the rear. The clientele, at least during the week, is a melting pot of Ukrainians, Poles, Mexicans, and Puerto Ricans; on weekends, the young professionals and artists—the recent arrivals—come to play pool. Every Thanksgiving and Christmas, Liacopoulos serves his patrons a turkey dinner.

Guinan and I take a seat at the bar. "Used to be packed with mailmen before they went to work," Guinan tells me. The local post office is the bar's neighbor, and while the postal workers come in less frequently, they still appear for the occasional shot and a beer. Guinan was reluctant to meet me here because in the early 1990s, a local weekly at Guinan's suggestion had written about the bar, and what was written—that it was a dive—angered the tavern's owners. This is the first time he's been back since that article, but all seems to have been forgiven: Liacopoulos greets him warmly. Guinan orders a Zywiec, a Polish beer, and—although he says he's stopped smoking—pulls out a pack of Marlboros. "I'm smoking now just 'cause I'm in a bar," he explains.

For nearly thirty years, Guinan drank and smoked and sketched at taverns around the city. He painted prostitutes and junkies, recent immigrants and blues singers. And he ventured out into the streets as well. He met an aging jazz piano player, Emile, who because of his musical prowess was known as the King of Clark Street; one of Guinan's paintings is of Emile sitting in his home, shoulders hunched, stomach flabby, playing his piano naked. Another of his subjects was Sister Carrie, an evangelist, who could usually be found at the Maxwell Street Market on Sunday mornings, jumping and shaking as she sang and banged on her tambourine. He captured people riding the El, sleeping and gazing out the window. He painted two boys climbing out of Lake Michigan under the shimmering light of street lamps. There's one painting in which, like voyeurs, we peek through the windows of the Fine Arts Building downtown, watching lithe young ballerinas in leotards and tutus practicing their routines. He drew a portrait of Mike, who ran a small dry cleaners that had become a neighborhood gathering spot, and he painted the women who used the back of Mike's shop to clean vegetables. He sketched the regal-looking African-American poet Margaret Danner, and boxing night at the Union League Club, where men in white shirts and ties and women in evening gowns watch young black and Hispanic men pummel each other to the mat.

Guinan does everything from small pencil sketches to large oils, some of which sell for as much as sixty thousand dollars. Taken together, his work, which has been compared to Edward Hopper's, comprises an astonishing collective portrait of the city. Where Hopper painted with strong, luminous colors, Guinan's work is muted and filled with extraordinary detail. In one portrait of Sister Carrie at her home, you can make out the mismatched, makeshift drapes covering the window and the ripped, layered linoleum on the floor. Dressed in her white domestic's uniform from the hotel where she worked, Sister Carrie sits erect in a fragile-looking wooden chair, her tambourine in her lap. You can sense her economic struggles and her strong bearing. The *International Herald Tribune* once wrote that Guinan portrays "a world of desolate dignity." An art dealer I spoke with said of Guinan's work that it feels familiar—not the artistry, but the people and places. There's an intimacy about his portraits that lets you feel that you know, or think you know, his subjects.

Guinan's work, as you might have gathered, is quite popular, although not in Chicago, where he's virtually unknown. But in France.

GUINAN IS ORIGINALLY from upstate New York and served a three-year peacetime stint in the army in Tripoli and Ankara as a radio operator. There, he fancied himself a Toulouse-Lautrec and sketched local peasants, imitating Toulouse-Lautrec's nervous brush strokes, which he later abandoned for a more disciplined, naturalistic style. He arrived in Chicago in 1959 to attend the School of the Art Institute, and a friend took him to Maxwell Street, an introduction that altered his life. Maxwell Street may have been one of the most exhilarating, industrious, and productive open street bazaars in the world. Begun in 1874 by Jewish merchants (in the same neighborhood as Manny's), it gradually became a hodgepodge collection of Jews, Mexicans, and African-Americans. (In its later years, the kids I knew from the West Side referred to it as Jewtown, even though by then most of the merchants were black.) On Sunday mornings, blues musicians like Muddy Waters and Howlin' Wolf played on the sidewalks, plugging their amps into the adjacent apartment buildings. Old men sold weathered *National Geographic* magazines, used picture frames, rusted tools, and assorted hardware such as nails and screws. On occasion, you could find new clothes and phonographs, though it was best not to ask where they came from. Samuel and Raymond Popeil, who eventually went on to invent the Veg-O-Matic and the Pocket Fisherman, honed their salesmanship techniques at Maxwell Street by hawking kitchenware. Street vendors barbecued

Polish sausages and pig's-ear sandwiches over fires set in city trash cans. "It was like being in Turkey or Libya," Guinan says. "This open street market, all the ruckus." He produced from that time a series of paintings that captured the market in its last days, solitary figures peddling their merchandise, and yet despite the fact that its end was near, there's a joy and liveliness to these works. They're among my favorites.

When the Maxwell Street Market was finally shut down in the late 1990s (there's a new, more sanitized version now a few blocks east), Guinan was devastated. "I thought it was the end of the world," he recalls. "They're destroying what's lovely about the city all for what? For condos." This has become a theme for Guinan, a city disappearing, but he's been saying it now for thirty years and so one begins to wonder if that isn't simply the nature of urban landscapes, that they shift and erode over time. Guinan soon discovered the bars on Clark Street, what was then Skid Row, and then the taverns in Wicker Park, including Rite Liquors.

In the interim, Guinan was discovered by a French art dealer, Albert Loeb, who saw three of Guinan's paintings at an art show in Switzerland. "It was a total surprise," recalls Loeb. "It was realism. The first person I thought of was Courbet." Gustave Courbet was a nineteenth-century French painter who, in an age when most art was idealized and historical, drew everyday villagers, in Courbet's words, "as nature made them, without corrections." (I mentioned to Guinan the comparison, and he laughed. His work does mirror Courbet's, he said, except that the revolutionary Courbet saw his renderings as a political statement, which Guinan says "seems silly today.") When Loeb contacted Guinan, it turned out that Guinan had only five other paintings. Over the years, he had burned everything else. "I just figured I wasn't going anywhere," he says.

Loeb sold one of his first Guinans to François Mitterrand, who was the head of the Socialist Party at the time and who bought a portrait of Emile sitting in his apartment by a space heater. Guinan's paintings have since been purchased by museums in Lyon, Grenoble, and Paris. The French diplomatic corps display Guinan's paintings in their embassies around the world. Two French filmmakers have made documentaries of Guinan; one of them, titled *Division Street,* filmed Guinan at Rite Liquors. Most recently, the actor Johnny Depp, who lives in France, stumbled upon Guinan's work and purchased a portrait of a one-legged prostitute sitting at a bar called the J.N.L. (It was one of the rare occasions on which Guinan didn't get his subject's name; he ran out of money to pay her for her time.) Even Guinan's biggest collector, Allison Davis, a Chicago developer, discovered Guinan during a vacation in Paris.

In Chicago, he's essentially unknown. Unnoticed. Like an invisible man, he likes to say, citing the moniker penned by a local reporter. Only three Chicagoans own Guinan's work. He has never had an exhibition here. Even with an occasional story over the years in the local press about Guinan, recognition for his work in the city has been elusive at best. When in the mid-1990s, for instance, the Museum of Contemporary Art held a show of Chicago artists, Guinan wasn't included. And despite efforts by Loeb, no Chicago art dealer has ever represented him. When asked about this neglect, Guinan will let out an exaggerated sigh. He'll quote the only American review he's ever received, from the former *New York Times* art critic Hilton Kramer, who wrote, "He strikes this observer as an artist of distinctly limited gifts who makes his impression primarily on the basis of his timely and dramatic subject matter." The review appeared in 1972, and yet Guinan knows it by heart. I asked a local gallery owner, Alice Adam, why she thought he hadn't found a place here. "Well, have you ever met him?" she replied. "He's sort of a hermit, a bit of a loner. He's bitter. I don't think he pushes enough." A former gallery owner suggested that he's too self-denigrating.

Guinan seems resigned to his fate, a chronicler of Chicago for all but Chicagoans. There's a touch of drama to Guinan, and if you catch him on a bad day, he can, indeed, sound embittered. "Ask Algren," he once told me. "Chicago kills its own. You have to go to New York to be a success. That was Algren's complaint. Algren says Chicago isn't the second city, it's the secondhand city." Guinan admires Algren. He owns first editions of five of his books, and has read each of them at least twice. In his studio hangs a black-and-white photograph of Algren in an overcoat walking down Division Street on a wintry day. Algren's good friend and unofficial photographer, Art Shea, signed it: *For Guinan—Who knows where it's at.*

Not long ago, Guinan invited me to join him and Loeb during one of Loeb's periodic visits to Chicago. Guinan lives on the city's North Side in a three-flat. He and his wife live on the first floor; he rents the second, and he uses the third landing as his studio. The three of us walked to a nearby coffee shop. Loeb has kept a kind of video journal of Guinan, filming his lectures, filming his interviews, filming interviews with Guinan's subjects. The unspoken assumption is that someday someone might be interested in it.

Guinan's neglect seems to hit Loeb harder than it does Guinan himself. At one point in our conversation, Loeb recounts an encounter with the curator of a Chicago museum. "She said Bob had no impact on Chicago," he tells me, indignant at the slight. To which Guinan replies, "She's right, I haven't." But Loeb won't let it go. He tells me the story of how in the mid-1990s, the city's Cultural Center was planning an exhibition of Guinan's work, how exciting that was, and then how it all fell through. Loeb says he was never completely clear about the reason why. Maybe it was the money needed to ship Guinan's work back to Chicago from Paris. Maybe it was the fact that the Democratic Convention was to be held in the city that year, and barflies, naked piano players, and reclining prostitutes weren't exactly the image the city wanted to put forth. Or maybe they just lost interest. Loeb, who's dressed in a safari shirt, appears agitated. "Were you disappointed?" I ask Guinan, giving him an opening. "No," he replies. Loeb then tells me about a Chicago art dealer who once said of Guinan's paintings, "Who wants to look at these? These are the people who want to mug you." To which Guinan sighs.

The *International Herald Tribune* once suggested that the reason Guinan's work is viewed with some suspicion in America and more specifically in Chicago "may be motivated by the idea that his art is burdened with a social message." When I ask him about this charge, Guinan responds as he often does, by telling a story that at first blush seems to have nothing to do with the matter at hand. In the early 1960s, he recounts, he'd been invited to a black storefront church on the West Side where the small congregation planned to honor the church's pianist, Spencer Randolph. Guinan knew Randolph from the taverns where he'd play at night. During the ceremony, the minister told a story about a boy who saw a lightning bug. The boy wondered why the lightning bug lit up like that, so he asked his father. His father, who wasn't an educated man, could only think to reply, "It's just something in him." Then the minister went on. "People ask us why we sing, why we shout, why we fall out? It's just something in us." Days later, I realize that Guinan was really talking about himself. It's just something in him.

An admirer says, "He's so intuitive, everything's so obvious to him. It's all inside him." I once asked Guinan why he chooses the subjects he does. "I wish I could say something like the people in these bars are more honest, more down-to-earth, that they don't put on any airs. But it's not necessarily true. . . . In the end, you see, all it is is someone for people to look at." He's being somewhat disingenuous, but his point his clear: His work—unlike, say Courbet's—is not meant as a social statement.

Guinan is attracted to the unvarnished quality of those who have little left to lose. He has become friends with many of those he painted. He attended the wedding of one, Sybil, a former prostitute. He took Emile to France with him for an opening, and Loeb rented a piano so that Emile could play. (The film *Casablanca* was popular in France at the time, recalls Guinan, so everyone kept asking for "As Time Goes By," which Emile, accustomed to honoring requests, was happy to play.) Guinan and his wife regularly dined with Loretta, whom he drew at Rite Liquors. And he would visit Geraldine, a former prostitute, at her room in the Fullerton Hotel to help her with letters she was writing to a lover.

These men and women are, for him, what the city is all about: people getting by, people with nothing to hide. He admires their straightforwardness, their directness. In the monograph of his work, he recalls some of his encounters, including the time he approached a prostitute named Anita at a bar and offered to pay her hourly fee of twenty dollars if she'd let him sketch her. She agreed, and the two retired to a by-the-hour room at the Victor Hotel.

"Now, I want you to behave as if I were a date," Guinan told her. "Do whatever you do and I will stop you at some point and ask you to pose. Do you take off your clothes?"

"Take off my clothes! On a date? I usually wear pants, you know, slacks. And just take out one leg. You don't want to do me with no clothes on anyway, I got terrible stretch marks."

Guinan guessed her age at twenty, but Anita told him she was in fact thirty-two and had three children. Guinan had her pose lying on the hotel bed, in red panties and bra, her hands behind her head. She has a distant look about her, as if she'd rather be somewhere else, which is probably how she looks when she's performing her job.

"It would be a lot easier to fuck, wouldn't it?" Anita suggested.

"I got to do this work."

"Takes all kinds."

Guinan needed to return the next week to finish the drawing, and he asked Anita if they could get the same room. She simply told the clerk that she had a date who couldn't "make it" unless he was in the same room, a request that didn't seem to fluster the man behind the desk.

It's a story which seems meant to let us know that Guinan recognizes that, in the end, he's completely dependent on the goodwill of his subjects. He often worries that he has taken advantage of people who are down on their luck. One time, he went on a rant about white suburbanites slumming at South Side blues clubs: "There's something about it I don't like. Young white rock musicians from the suburbs will go down to some dark South Side neighborhood and have themselves photographed against some bleak urban setting to make it look as if they live there, as if they suffered the hard knocks. They've taken someone else's misfortune to use as a background for their own mediocrity." "But couldn't people say that about you?" I asked. "Exactly. Exactly. 'Cause I feel like in the back of my mind I'm doing something similar . . . I mean I pay them, but in a way I get that nagging feeling that maybe I'm exploiting these people." "Is that why you stopped doing it?" "No, I stopped doing it 'cause my stomach was killing me. It got to the point two years ago that I couldn't stand looking at another beer."

BUT GUINAN HAS another problem. His subjects are moving targets. Gentrification has pushed the poor and the marginalized this way, then that. It's like being rocked on a ship. First Maxwell Street closed. Then Clark Street was cleaned up, and then the artists and young financiers moved into Wicker Park, and gone were the taverns, the King Palace, the J.N.L., and Sam's. Rite Liquors is one of the last of his hangouts still standing. "The image of Chicago is becoming self-conscious," he says. "Suddenly

the mayor wants to clean it up, make it look like Anywhere, USA, with a lot of wrought-iron fences and flowers. Flowers in all the parking lots. There seems to be this
need to homogenize the place. It was a city of neighborhoods but more and more it's becoming . . ." He doesn't
finish his thought. He doesn't have to.

Guinan's still painting. He's been sketching jazz and
blues musicians at places like the HotHouse and the Velvet
Lounge. He can depend on them. They're predictable. He
knows when they'll be there. He tired of the chase. We
met up one night at the Velvet Lounge, a small, dark former speakeasy with floral-print wallpaper from the 1940s.
On the wall opposite the bar are photographs of jazz musicians who have played here. On one of them, the soprano
saxophonist Steve Lacy has scrawled, *This place is a temple.*
The lounge is owned by saxophonist Fred Anderson,
who's now in his seventies and, as the founder of a modern
jazz co-op, has performed here and overseas, in Germany,
Hungary, France, and Japan. Someday, Guinan wants to
paint a portrait of Anderson, whose curved posture resem-
bles a sax. Guinan had taken me here this particular evening to hear Nichole Mitchell, a jazz flutist whom he has
painted. He titled one of the portraits "Wheat Grass,"
since for a while Mitchell lived on a diet of wheat grass. (A
French pharmacist bought that work.) There were six
members of the band, and nine of us in the audience, not
counting two middle-aged men at the bar watching a
Chicago Bulls game. When we returned to the Lounge

a few weeks later, this time to hear Edward Wilkerson, Jr., a young, talented sax player who's been reviewed in *The Atlantic Monthly* and whose pieces are, as Guinan suggests, like individual short stories, the crowd again was scarce—three people besides ourselves. "That's why I identify with these guys, 'cause I don't have an audience either," he says.

There's a touch of self-pity in his voice, but I've become convinced over time that Guinan wouldn't have it any other way. To be recognized now in his city would mean he'd have to rewrite his own story. A friend with whom he's had a falling out says of his outsider status: "I guess I always thought that was just part of his personality. I guess my point is that not being appreciated in Chicago is largely a deliberate thing. Van Gogh was anguished over [not being appreciated in France]. He was terribly unhappy about it. That's probably why he killed himself. But it's the way Bob wants it. . . . It's by design." Loeb told me, out of Guinan's earshot, that perhaps Guinan's obscurity in his native city is necessary: "That's the way he looks at society, as an outsider."

For all of Algren's affection for and reliance on Chicago, he became more and more embittered by the rejection of his hometown. In an afterword he wrote ten years after the initial publication of *City on the Make,* he wrote: "Love is by remembrance. Unlike the people of Paris or London or New York or San Francisco, who prove their love by recording their times in paintings and plays and books and films and poetry, the lack of love of Chicagoans for

Chicago stands self-evident by the fact that we make no living record of it here."

But of course that's precisely what Guinan has done. He's expressed his love by remembrance. For all of Guinan's identification with Algren, he lacks the author's bluster and harshness. In a moment of candor, he told me, "I feel so damn lucky I'm appreciated somewhere. And it's so damn nice to walk down a street in Chicago and nobody knows who I am. The whole thing's an accident. Somebody from Europe liked my work and that's why I'm there."

It still doesn't explain why Guinan hasn't found a place in his hometown, why he isn't more celebrated here. Those I spoke with suggested that it must be the subject matter. Too depressing. Too dark. Too desolate. When we were at Rite Liquors, I asked Guinan what seemed to me the obvious question: "Why not move to Paris, where you're loved?" But Paris, he told me, is too pretty. "It'd be like living your life in a pastry shop," says Guinan. "What can you paint in Paris?" He took another swig of his Zywiec.

Inside Out

*You are gigantic in your virtues and gigantic in your
vices. I don't know in which you glory the most.*

> *British journalist* WILLIAM T. SNEAD,
> *on visiting Chicago in 1893*

PERIODICALLY, DAVE BOYLE LEAVES LONG, RAM-
bling messages on my voice mail. He usually starts off
by saying, "Alex, I thought you'd enjoy this." He then pro-
ceeds to recount some perceived act of lunacy (or larceny)
that's occurred in his hometown of Cicero. There was one
occasion, though, after the town's president was indicted,
when he left an uncharacteristically brief message, his glee
undisguised: "Alex, 'Ding Dong! The witch is dead.' " In
fact, that was the first of two times he left that particular
greeting. But I'm getting ahead of myself here.

Dave Boyle is a gadfly, a persistent, irritating, in-your-face critic of the powers that be in Cicero. I understand that this is a book about Chicago, about the city proper, but it's impossible to talk about the city without speaking of the suburbs. Unlike New York, where the suburbs feel as if they might as well be on the other side of the Hudson River (which, in New Yorkese, means a not inconsiderable distance), or in Los Angeles, where the city feels like an illegitimate child left behind by the sprawl, Chicago's first ring of burghs are, in truth, extensions of the city. The city moves outward from Lake Michigan, and as you venture north, south, or, in Cicero's case, west, you seamlessly and unknowingly cross into these small towns which feel more urban than suburban. Indeed, the city's transit line extends into a number of them. Street names often remain the same. (I live in Oak Park, four blocks from the city's border, a block from the El, and down the street from a building that houses teachers from a Chicago elementary school.) Cicero, a town of small brick bungalows, narrow streets, and manufacturing plants, is almost indistinguishable from the city's West Side neighborhoods, and this working-class community's history is deeply intertwined with Chicago's. But finally the story of Cicero is a story of Chicago's tribalism: For years, it was a town run by insiders who successfully fought to keep the world at bay.

Dave and his wife, Nadine, bought a home in Cicero in 1983; Dave was a contractor and the town seemed to be on the verge of new development, so he thought it would be a good place to ply his trade. Within the first year of their stay, he was on his way to a job early one morning when he pulled out of an alley and saw a rough-looking crowd outside Mr. C's, a local tavern frequented by the Chicago branch of the Outlaws motorcycle gang. It quickly became clear that someone had been murdered. Boyle could make out the chalk lines of a body, and the police were gathering evidence. As for the gang members, they were on the sidewalk, drinking beer and celebrating: There had been a fight and the best man, at least in the eyes of the surviving Outlaws, had won. Boyle pulled over, got out of his car, and asked what had happened. "The police told me that the guy had been stabbed inside, and while he was still bleeding from a gut cut from a buck knife, gurgling blood, these bikers carried him out of Mr. C's onto the street so he'd die out there," Boyle recalls. It became clear that the bikers had moved the dying man to keep the bar from getting shut down, even temporarily, and it also quickly became apparent that police had obliged them. Mr. C's was still serving beer.

Boyle decided that Cicero would be a better place to live if Mr. C's, which had a history of wild brawls, was closed down, so he went to see the village's deputy liquor commissioner. The commissioner told Boyle that there was nothing he could do about Mr. C's, and that if Boyle knew what was good for him, he wouldn't mention it again. But Boyle, who's not easily discouraged, returned six days later, and this time the deputy commissioner was more blunt. He told Boyle that if Boyle did anything about Mr. C.'s, not only might they kill Boyle but they might kill him, as well. The "they" he was referring to was organized crime.

"I just basically thought, 'Fuck you. I'm Dave Boyle,' " Boyle told me. "I walk upright, and I ask you to do the right thing, and you tell me the mob won't let you do it. I thought, 'What kind of pussy are you?' "

THERE ARE PROBABLY a few things you need to know about Cicero. First, if you haven't already figured this out, it's a tough little town. It always has been. I was once interviewed by a reporter from Japan, and Cicero came up in the conversation: The reporter pulled his index fingers out of his imaginary holsters and started shooting. This gesture has become the town's international symbol, because as almost everyone knows—especially foreigners, who seem particularly obsessed with America's gangster tradition—this was for a while the home of Al Capone, America's most legendary gangster.

When William Dever was elected mayor of Chicago in 1923, he announced that, unlike his predecessor, he intended to enforce Prohibition, and he vowed to crush "the rumrunners and illicit beer peddlers." So, Capone, who was only twenty-five and still a relatively unknown small-time hoodlum, moved his operations to Cicero. It was a town, writes Laurence Bergreen in his biography of Capone, "small enough for the organization to control.

They could *own* the city government, from the mayor to the dog catcher . . . and indeed, the big city merged almost imperceptibly into its smaller neighbor."

Capone opened gambling dens and brothels in Cicero, and began fixing races at the Hawthorne racetrack (which still exists). He set up shop first at the Anton Hotel, and then at the more substantial Hawthorne Hotel; he also owned a small apartment building on Austin Avenue, where he'd take his mistresses and hold all-night parties. While it was rumored to have an escape tunnel leading from the building to the garage, Capone's operations were considerably more low-tech, and indeed he exerted such control in places like Cicero that he had no need for hideouts. (His home, where his wife and mother lived, was a rather modest dwelling on Chicago's South Side, on the 7200 block of South Prairie Avenue.) In October 1924, Capone commandeered the local Cicero elections with a brutal show of force: His henchmen kidnapped poll workers, one of whom was murdered. On that same day, Al's brother Frank was gunned down by Chicago policemen who had been deputized to work the election. Although Capone's slate won, Bergreen writes that "the death of Frank became a turning point in Capone's career as a racketeer. From now on he would become the dedicated outlaw, determined to crush and control." Capone operated out of Cicero until Dever lost his election four years later to the highly corrupt "Big Bill" Thompson, whose campaign was in part financed by racketeers including Capone.

(One of Thompson's favorite nightspots was Ralph Capone's Cotton Club in Cicero.) Capone moved his base of operations back to Chicago but continued to have a significant presence in Cicero until he went to prison in 1932.

It's a connection that irritates townsfolk, especially because it's always the first thing the media has to say about this place. In 1953, Cicero considered changing its name because, the town's lawyer said, "People everywhere think we're just a bunch of hoods. A kid from Cicero can't get into a college fraternity." As recently as 1993, still hoping to divert reporters from the Capone association, the town raised banners that claimed Cicero was THE ORIGINAL BIRTH- PLACE OF ERNEST HEMINGWAY. Hemingway actually hailed from nearby Oak Park, which in 1899 was unincorporated and therefore technically—if not socially—a part of Cicero.

Defensiveness about Capone is understandable, but it seems misplaced only because the other reason for Cicero's notoriety is by most measures considerably more embarrassing. Plainly and simply, for decades Cicero had a policy of no blacks allowed. It was as intense and as forceful as anything seen in the pre–civil rights South. I would venture to guess that the town was among the most adept in the nation at keeping out African-Americans. For many years, the village refused to take certain federal grants so that it wouldn't have to comply with open housing or hiring laws. Lithuanians and Italians who grew up there have told me that as kids they would run any black they saw out of town—at the behest of the police. In 1951, Illinois's governor, Adlai Stevenson, had to call in the National Guard when for three days a mob threw rocks and chunks of metal into the second-floor apartment of a black bus driver and his family who had just moved in. With town cops looking on (and some allegedly supplying rocks), these Ciceroans eventually stormed the apartment and threw the family's belongings out the window, including their piano. When Martin Luther King, Jr., in 1967 had come to Chicago to lead his open-housing campaign, he announced he'd march in Cicero, a move meant to embarrass Chicago's Mayor Daley, who had resisted Dr. King's efforts. But when county officials told King they couldn't guarantee his safety, he chose not to march, this after having faced the likes of Sheriff Bull Conner in Birmingham. King referred to Cicero as the Selma of the North. And then, in the 1980s, after a run-in between a police sergeant and one of the few African-American families who'd moved to Cicero, the Justice Department ordered the police to undergo race sensitivity training. My father-in-law, Jack, helped lead those workshops, and he recalled one police sergeant attending a session in a T-shirt that read POLICE BRUTALITY. THE FUN PART OF POLICE WORK.

THIS IS WHAT Boyle walked into when he moved here, but initially he and Cicero seemed like a fair match. Boyle, who was a Marine in Vietnam, is built like a rugby player, squat and broad-shouldered. He has a bulldog of a face, ruddy and pug-nosed. When he gets angry, his hands instinctively ball into fists. He says things that he probably shouldn't, and he often doesn't know when to retreat. Once, after a town meeting, a man who looked half Boyle's age stared at Boyle in the hallway. "What you staring at?" Boyle growled. "Bite my fuckin' ass."

"Fuck you," the younger man replied.

"Fuck you," Boyle replied, pushing up against the man. Boyle's body tensed, his hands, it seemed, preparing to make contact. "Outside," he suggested.

It was the young man, not Boyle, who knew enough to walk away.

After being told by the deputy liquor commissioner that it would be best if he kept quiet, Boyle did just the opposite: He convinced nearly four hundred of his neighbors to show up at a city council meeting and got the town to shut down Mr. C's. He then collected enough signatures for an advisory referendum that called for all bars to close at two a.m. Voters passed the measure, three to one, but the town president refused to rescind the current closing time of six a.m. So Boyle went through town records and found that five bars, which he believed to be run by the mob, hadn't bothered to renew their liquor licenses. He then went to the police department to lodge a complaint.

That night, at two a.m., he and Nadine were woken by a blast. Dave looked out of his second-floor bedroom window and saw his garage in flames. Someone had blown it up. By the time the fire department extinguished the blaze, Boyle had lost his garage, his construction tools, and his two cars, a van and a Volkswagen Beetle. Then the threats began. "Guys used to call me at night," he recalled. "They'd tell me they were going to kill me, that they were going to fuck my wife, and I'd call them homosexuals and tell them that my light on my porch is on, that my door's open, that if you guys got the balls to come over, come on over. My wife's in a very attractive nightie right now. You might like it." And then one day Boyle went to get his newspaper, and draped across his porch railing he found a decapitated snake.

Boyle was pretty much on his own. The police were far more interested in harassing Boyle than in finding out who was harassing him. Again and again, over the next few years, they arrested him, eleven times in all, once for defending himself against a rowdy drunk, another time for forcefully escorting home a teenage bully who had been hassling some girls. Nadine, who is as softspoken as Dave is loud, would have to borrow money from neighbors to bail Dave out until she finally caught on and stored cash in the house. What was hardest for Nadine is that there was no one to turn to. "I didn't talk to my friends anymore because I felt different than they did," she told me. "They were having babies. They were decorating their houses with Laura Ashley things and I'm cleaning up ashes from the garage." The paranoia began to get to her. "There was a man in the alley behind our house, he had urine stains on his pants, he had three-day-old newspapers in his hands, he had on gym shoes and a funny hat. He told me he was an undercover guy for the CIA. And I'm sure that's what I sounded like to my friends. And then there was a point where I started to believe that guy. I didn't know anymore. That was a sign we needed to move on."

Boyle insists he wasn't run out of town, but Nadine, in particular, began to fear for her husband's safety. In 1990, they moved to Houston, where Boyle had an uncle, and they purchased a comfortable ranch house with a swimming pool. Boyle went to law school. They had a good life there. Nadine said they laughed together, they could relax. But one day, some ten years later, Dave told Nadine that he wanted to return to Cicero, that it didn't feel right not being there. She felt sick. She told Dave it was as if he'd hit her with a board. But she knew her husband well enough to recognize that he was going stir-crazy, that even Texas politics didn't hold a candle to what they'd been up against in Cicero. And so they moved back, bought a small bungalow, and reentered the fray. "I just wanted to finish up business," he told me.

WHEN DAVE AND NADINE returned in the summer of 2000, Cicero had undergone a remarkable transformation. During their absence, this town of insiders—Lithuanians, Bohemians, and Italians—had been overrun by outsiders. Cicero had remained fairly successful at keeping out blacks, but slowly, and then in large numbers, Hispanics had moved in—so many, in fact, that by the time the Boyles returned Hispanics made up three-fourths of the population. ("Well, they're not black," one resident told me by way of explaining why Hispanics had been permitted to settle in the town.) Yet, the town was still run by the old guard.

Shortly after the Boyles had left for Texas, Betty Loren-Maltese had been elected town president. At the time, she was the wife of Frank Maltese, who was the town assessor as well as bookmaker for then Cicero mob boss Rocco Infelice. (Frank Maltese died of cancer before going off to prison, in 1993.) In the intervening years, Loren-Maltese had become one of the most recognizable politicians in all of Illinois. She honed a look that harked back to the 1950s, and I suspect that the association was not unintentional. (Loren-Maltese said at one point, "I want things like they used to be.") A full-figured woman, she wore her hair in a pompadour and wore lengthy false eyelashes coated in thick black mascara. Reporters often noted a passing resemblance to Elizabeth Taylor. She favored brilliantly colored pantsuits and wore her electric-blue version to court on at least one occasion. She was highly quotable when she agreed to speak with the press, which wasn't often, and also highly combustible—which is why her handlers tried to keep her away from those intent on recording her every word. A Chicago columnist once wrote, "She's a headline."

Loren-Maltese named the town's public safety building after her late husband, a convicted felon. When in 1998 the Ku Klux Klan announced plans to march through town, she raised ten thousand dollars to pay them to cancel the rally. She took on the street gangs with heavy-handed—the ACLU said illegal—tactics, which included impounding the cars of suspected gang members. But because Loren-Maltese was often a source of amusement for outsiders, her shrewdness as a politician was underestimated. She included Hispanics in her administration and was reelected twice over the course of ten years, once defeating an Hispanic opponent by a two-to-one margin. Moreover, in the venerable Cicero tradition, she had irregular but effective ways of quieting her critics.

Once, when a priest, Father Jim Kastigar, complained about treatment of Hispanics in the town—town officials had ordered a bank that flew a Mexican flag to lower it, and police allegedly would regularly shake down Mexican-Americans for money if they didn't have a green card—he had his permit denied to hold the annual Way of the Cross procession, a Mexican Catholic tradition. Then the town closed down the church's kitchen because, officials claimed, they were running a food business without a license. (A church youth group had been selling tamales.) And then the town cut off parking access to the public school across the street, which had always left its lot open for church-goers on Sunday. "Cicero," one resident said at the time, "is like the twilight zone."

—⁓—

WHEN I FIRST MET BOYLE, he'd just come back to town, and his spirits were high. He referred to Loren-Maltese in terms that probably are best left out of print. "What do you plan to do?" I asked. "I'm applying for a building permit," he said.

"No," I tried to clarify. "What are you going to do to go after Loren-Maltese?"

He laughed. "Apply for a building permit."

"I don't understand," I told him.

"I'll mandamus them," he said. He planned to sue them. Boyle was going to prick them every chance he got. When an Hispanic candidate challenged Loren-Maltese for reelection, the candidate was followed home from a party and arrested for driving under the influence. Boyle thought it was a setup, and so he filed a Freedom of Information Act request for the arrest reports. And he would show up at city council meetings, where he'd badger Loren-Maltese and address her as "Madam President," drawing out the syllables, his voice mockingly reverential, as if she were a Third World despot. Once at a town meeting, he urged her to resign, to which she snapped, "Why don't you shut up and let the people speak."

When David Niebur, a former police chief, sued the town and Loren-Maltese for wrongfully firing him, Dave and Nadine appeared at every day of the trial, taking notes. Dave identified with Niebur, who had also taken on Cicero's powers, and, like Dave, had suffered the consequences. Niebur had made the mistake of responding to citizen complaints about the town's aggressive towing policy. The town had been towing roughly eighteen thousand vehicles a year, and shortly before Niebur had arrived, the town had awarded its sole towing contract—at five hundred dollars a tow, a lucrative deal—to a newly incorporated company that Niebur began to suspect had ties to town officials. The FBI apparently had similar suspicions, and Niebur soon was subpoenaed to testify before a grand jury. Then Niebur caught one of the tow firm's owners rifling through police records. Niebur turned over the department's towing records to the state police and to the FBI.

One of the things that doesn't go down well with Cicero's establishment is assisting the feds, the penultimate outsiders. Niebur testified that the town attorney at one point said to him, "You're not cooperating with those fuckin' assholes, are you?" A few days later, Loren-Maltese fired Niebur and publicly called him "stupid" and a "nitwit." Niebur also testified that when his belongings were sent to him, among them was a figurine of a police officer holding the hand of a lost boy. It had been a gift from his nephew. The head of the police officer had been twisted off and laid neatly next to the statue in the Styrofoam packing. Niebur, who had returned to his hometown of Joplin, Missouri, was awarded $1.7 million.

Within the year, Loren-Maltese was brought up on charges of pilfering more than twelve million dollars from the town, along with a troika of alleged mob-connected men and another former chief of police. It appears that all along, at least in the short time Boyle had been back, Loren-Maltese had been under investigation. She was convicted, and her attorneys pleaded with the judge for a lenient sentence, especially because Loren-Maltese was a single parent to her five-year-old daughter. But it was soon disclosed that Loren-Maltese had wagered a staggering eighteen million dollars in casinos, suggesting that she may well have spent more time gambling than she did parenting. The judge sentenced her to eight years and one month, and it was then that Boyle called me and left the second message, " 'Ding Dong! The witch is dead.' " And then in a voice meant to mimic Loren-Maltese's, " 'I'm melting. I'm melting.' "

BOYLE IS NOW practicing law out of his home, except on Saturday mornings, when he runs a legal clinic at the town's Democratic offices, a storefront along one of the town's commercial boulevards. It's a bare room, narrow but deep; Boyle meets with his clients in a cubicle in the rear. He invited me to join him one Saturday morning. His clientele, he told me, are a mix of old immigrants and new, a cascade of outsiders. They come to Boyle when they have nowhere else to turn, and while Boyle tries to keep an arm's distance, he inevitably gets swallowed up by some of the stories he hears. He is, after all, an angry man, and so he can and does get angry on behalf of the people he represents.

Boyle's first client is a forty-year-old political refugee from Lithuania. Valdos (he asked that I not use his last name) is dressed in a fire-engine-red shirt, black shorts, white socks, and loafers. He has a pink earring in his left ear. He looks like a working-class version of Liberace. He's been in this country for thirteen years, and he buys and sells jewelry, which explains the magnifying glass hanging from his neck. Valdos wanted to purchase a two-flat, and one of his tenants, a white gentleman, hasn't paid rent for six months; Valdos wants to know how easy it would be to evict him. Cicero, Boyle tells me, has a big problem with deadbeat tenants, usually white, who know that landlords will initially favor them over Hispanics. Urban nomads, they move from one apartment to the next, often getting six months of free rent. Boyle tells Valdos that for a hundred dollars plus the filing fees he'd help file an eviction notice.

Enriquez, who's twenty-six years old and has been laid off as a delivery man for Miller beer, arrives with his father, Tony, who was the first Mexican-American precinct captain in the town. Enriquez tells Boyle his story. Six weeks ago, he says, he called the police because a gaggle of gang members loitering on his block pulled out guns. Three times that night, the police came, but each time the gang members had disappeared into the alleys and walkways. Enriquez admits he got a bit heated, and he said to

one of the officers, "Why don't you do your job, man?"
Well, the other night, Enriquez goes on, he had dropped
off a friend in an unfamiliar part of town, and to get home
he drove down an alley, where he got stopped by that same
officer. Enriquez didn't have his insurance card, and so his
car, a 1995 Buick LeSabre, was towed. Boyle asks for the
officer's name. Enriquez tells him. "Oh, shit," says Boyle.
"He ain't never seen an Hispanic who he doesn't think is a
criminal. He's a prick." Boyle instructs Enriquez not to
pay the seven-hundred-fifty-dollar towing fee since if he
does he has to waive his rights to contest the claim. Boyle
tells him that for a hundred dollars he can help him beat
the charge. "You got the balls to do this?" Boyle asks.
Enriquez hesitates. His wife works as a bank teller, and she
needs the car to get to work. His father tells him he'll lend
his car to Enriquez. Boyle claps his hands. "Then we're
done. It's the only way the shit stops."

A twenty-seven-year-old Hispanic woman, Gabriella,
who works for the Department of Public Aid, arrives with
her seven-year-old daughter and her mother. She's concerned that her father's death from a blood clot could have
been avoided if he hadn't initially been wrongly diagnosed
at a local hospital. Boyle tells her he doesn't handle personal injury lawsuits. While they're talking, they realize
that Gabriella was taught by Boyle's sister in seventh grade.
And then Gabriella lays out her other problems. A black
tenant hasn't paid his rent for three months. "And the
thing is," Gabriella says, "my daughter's father is black. I'm

not the kind of person to put a copy on someone, but . . ." This reminds her that she wants to take her daughter to Mexico. Does she need the father's permission even if he hasn't seen their daughter in three years? she asks. Boyle tells her to bring in the rental agreement, and assures her that she can take her daughter to Mexico. Then her mother, who only speaks Spanish, reminds Gabriella that the city wants her to tear down her garage because it's in disrepair. Boyle realizes they could go on. He leans over the circular table and in an uncharacteristically soft voice says, "Gabriella, I have an office full of people."

Indeed, the waiting room is now so crowded, there aren't enough seats for everyone. There's a middle-aged Hispanic woman whose common-law husband kicked her out of the house for another woman and is now trying to get custody of their three sons. ("If I get that sonofabitch in court and don't kill him it'll be a miracle," Boyle tells her.) There's a construction worker whose wife left him two years ago and took their two young children; he wants to find a way to see them again. And there's another land-lord whose tenants are behind in the rent.

Boyle hollers out to someone to lock the doors. If he doesn't, he worries, he'll be here all day. He turns to me. "If I didn't have Cicero," he says, "I don't know what I'd do."

A FEW WEEKS LATER, Boyle suggests we meet for lunch at Freddy's, a storefront Italian market on 16th Street in

Cicero. Boyle orders for the two of us: fried pork sand-wiches. He then buys lunch for two women, a court bailiff and a deputy sheriff. He tells me later that their favor might come in handy someday. We find a table on the sidewalk as an older man emerges from a van with the town's insignia on the side. "Water department," Boyle says to me. "Just another sleazy bag man for the mob." The "sleazy bag man for the mob" walks by, and he and Boyle exchange friendly greetings. "Freddy's is a neutral place," Boyle tells me. "Good guys. Bad guys. Intellectuals. Thugs. Politicians. Cops. Freddy's puts us all at our best."

Freddy's has been around since the 1940s, when it was owned by a Dutch man who named the restaurant after his father. Joe Quercia purchased it in 1973. He was eighteen, and only five years earlier had come over from Naples. Originally, it was simply a corner grocery store, but then Quercia and his wife, Anne Marie, whom he had met when she came in for a slice of pizza, realized that they couldn't compete with the larger supermarket chains. And so the Quercias turned the place into a small specialty shop: everything Italian. Quercia makes his own pasta, as well as Italian ices (from natural fruit juices) and gelatos. He also makes *arancine*—ground meat and peas wrapped in cooked rice, then deep-fried for a few minutes. And he sells pan pizza by the slice, which has never been easy to find in Chicago.

In the 1980s, the area's top mobsters ate here, including Anthony "Big Tuna" Accardo, an enforcer for Capone who later took over Chicago's syndicate, personally controlling ten thousand gambling dens. (Though never convicted of any crimes, he had a fierce reputation; when, in 1977, six men burglarized his River Forest home, all of them were eventually tracked down and murdered, their throats slashed.) Meals at Freddy's were never disturbed, however. "They never bothered me," Quercia told me. "They always paid. Once I tried to offer a free lemonade to Joey Aiuppo [Accardo's second in command] 'cause he brought me some doves and pheasants that he'd bagged hunting. But he insisted on paying. Always a gentleman." Frank Maltese, Betty's husband, came here almost every day for a lemon or watermelon ice when he was undergoing chemotherapy treatments. One incarcerated mobster so liked Quercia's homemade Italian bread that he had his son smuggle slices into the prison stashed in potato chip bags.

Firefighters and police often get takeout here. While I'm eating with Boyle, a hook-and-ladder truck pulls up from Berwyn, a neighboring town, and one of the firemen runs in to pick up lunches for his colleagues back at the firehouse. "I don't think they're supposed to bring their trucks over here," Quercia whispers. Boyle's cell phone rings. It's his wife, Nadine. She still worries that if she hasn't heard from him it means he's been arrested by the police. "I'm all right," Boyle assures. "Love ya." A retired Cicero police officer enters the store, and while he and Boyle don't exchange greetings, they don't holler at each other either—which, all things considered, is progress. A few weeks back, they had gotten into it at the town hall. "You're nothing but a goddamn lawyer," the retired officer had yelled at Boyle. "At least you didn't call me a fuckin' Cicero cop," Boyle had yelled back.

Boyle recounts this exchange as the retired officer exits. They acknowledge each other with barely perceptible nods. "You know," Boyle tells me. "I can't even remember what we were arguing about."

GT's Diner

THE WORLD INTERSECTS AT THE CORNER OF LAW-
rence and Kedzie Avenues, on the city's northwest
side.

The names of the commercial establishments read like
an intercontinental guidebook. Within a three-block stretch,
there is Raul's Tire Shop and a Supermercado, there is Holy
Land Baker and Jerusalem Food and Liquor, there is
Jas Hind Grocery, New Seoul Optical, Thai Little Home
Café, and Patricia Cowboy's Fashion. More than half the
people in this neighborhood, which is known as Albany
Park, were born in a foreign country. This is America's
gateway, the port of entry for newcomers to this country.
For small merchandisers, the biggest-selling item is phone
calling cards. One establishment sells *only* calling cards.
The local Volta Elementary School offers bilingual classes
in Spanish, Gujarati, Arabic, Vietnamese, and Bosnian. Six
clocks in the hallway are set to the times in Sarajevo, Lima,

Jerusalem, New Delhi, Hanoi, and Chicago. Albany Park, one resident told me, "is the neighborhood for everybody else who doesn't have a neighborhood."

For half a century, this community of wood-framed homes, brick bungalows, and three- and four-story tenements was home to mostly Russian and Eastern European Jews. Then in the 1960s, Koreans moved in, and they became such a political force that Lawrence Avenue was given the honorary designation of Seoul Drive. Then immigrants from unraveling nations poured in, refugees from Guatemala and El Salvador, families fleeing the fragile Mexican economy, and then Laotians, Thais, Cambodians, and Filipinos fleeing the political instability of their homelands, and finally refugees from Iran, Iraq, Lebanon, and Yemen. By this time, many of Albany Park's original settlers had moved on. Temple Beth Israel first was converted into a Korean Presbyterian church and is now a Romanian Pentecostal church. Congregation Mount Sinai became, not without irony, the Beirut Restaurant. From Albany Park, it has been suggested, you can watch the world change.

The neighborhood has the feel of a small village, in part because the El runs at street level, like a trolley, making the community quite accessible. But it's also because virtually everyone here shares a common journey: They have come to Chicago, to America, for a better life. And so an amalgam of ethnic and religious groups mingles in a manner unlike the city's other more insular neighborhoods. At Thai Little Home Café, for instance, the owner, Oscar Esche, who is seventy-seven and has been in this country and this neighborhood since 1972, doesn't serve pork since many of his customers are Middle Eastern and Muslim. The Cambodian Association on Lawrence Avenue is building a small memorial to the victims of the Khmer Rouge, and they are doing so with the financial and moral support of the Jewish community. Jewish leaders—some of whom grew up in Albany Park—have spoken with members of the Cambodian Association about how one moves on after the decimation of one's people. And at the Albany Park Theater Group, teenagers from places as diverse as Poland and Cambodia come together twice a year to perform a play based on stories of those in the community.

Albany Park is also a place where America is celebrated, often in a rather self-conscious manner. Each Thanksgiving, Esche sets up a full turkey dinner in his backyard, as an offering to Abraham Lincoln. "In our culture," Esche tells me, "you were brought up to pay respect to the king, so here we pay respect to Lincoln. He's like one of our kings in Thailand who freed the slaves, King Rama V." (In his restaurant, he displays a bust of Lincoln and a poster-size photo of this turn-of-the-century monarch.) Also, each spring Esche and his family—his wife, his wife's sister, and his three children—drive four hours to Springfield to visit Lincoln's tomb, where they kneel and offer thanks for what they have.

Down the street from Esche's restaurant is Mataam Al-

Mataam, which is Arabic for "Restaurant–Restaurant."
Open twenty-four hours, it's owned by Kamel Botres, who
emigrated from Iraq in 1979. Botres, who is Catholic, had
worked as a clerk for a private oil company in his home-
land. During the 2003 invasion of Iraq, and then again
when Saddam Hussein was captured, local television reporters descended on Mataam Al-Mataam, seeking reac-
tions to what had just occurred halfway around the globe.
In the case of Saddam's capture, many of the customers—
they come from throughout the Middle East and North
Africa (though the young waitresses are from Venezuela,
Romania, and Pakistan)—told reporters that they didn't
believe it was actually him. And even those, like Botres,
who didn't have any doubts that the United States had the
right man were subdued. "People felt a little sorry. It was
their president. You'd feel that way if it was your president," Botres said. "There was nothing to celebrate." He
smiles as he tells me this. "I am an American in my heart,"
he told me. "I can think how I want."

I MENTION ALL THIS by way of introduction, to Ramazan
Celikoski, the owner of GT's, a diner located half a mile
west of Mataam Al-Mataam and the Thai Little Home
Café, just down the street from the Bohemian National
Cemetery, where Mayor Cermak is buried. GT's is a
rather compact place—eight stools at the counter and five
booths along the wall—and is situated at the end of a small

strip mall, which also houses a Laundromat, a liquor store, and a pizza parlor. In the diner's plate-glass windows hang five signs, all in different fonts and colors, one of them handwritten, each at a different angle. BREAKFAST one advertises. 3 EGGS, HASH BROWNS AND TOAST. $2.75.

Celikoski (pronounced *Chelikoski*) was twenty years old in 1982 when he left Albania for the United States. His father, who had had a sheep farm in Albania and had fled after his own father, an anti-Communist, had mysteriously disappeared, had preceded Ramazan by twelve years and was working as a cook in a downtown restaurant when Celikoski arrived. For a year, the two shared a room in a hotel, and then Ramazan found an apartment in Albany Park. Like his father, he worked in a series of eating establishments, as a busboy at a fancy downtown restaurant and as a cook at the popular coffee shop Lou Mitchell's. It was at his first job that coworkers began calling him John, which is what he goes by today. In the summer of 2003, he purchased GT's (truthfully, all he had to do was pick up the two-thousand-dollar-a-month lease) from a hot-tempered man, who also happened to be Albanian; while the previous owner had been losing money, Celikoski thought with his more easygoing nature he could turn it around. Though he did break even in his fourth month, he has yet to make a profit, in part because here, in this out-of-the-way strip mall, Celikoski has, grousing along the way, unintentionally transformed GT's into the equivalent of a domestic nongovernmental organization—an NGO.

Celikoski, who's forty-two and of medium build, has deep-set eyes, dark, thick eyebrows, and a hawklike nose, all of which might conspire to give him a look of intensity were it not for his ever-present crooked grin, which seems to say, "What are you going to do?" The first time we met, it was midafternoon, and the diner was empty except for two Mexican-American men in a nearby booth. "They're no good," he muttered, nodding toward the two patrons. "Some of them drink too much. Some of them are here from six in the morning until twelve and not even buy coffee. At lunchtime, I tell them they got to go." As he complained about the day laborers, he was, as always, smiling.

Shortly after Celikoski purchased GT's, a group of two hundred or so day laborers were evicted from the spot where they had been congregating each morning at a nearby bus turnaround. There they had constructed a make-shift plywood hut to give them shelter from the rain. They soon found their way over to GT's, where, because of the mall's parking lot, there was room for employers to drive in and pick up workers for the day. Moreover, the day laborers needed a place to take shelter from the elements as well as a bathroom. GT's offered both. On any given morning in the winter, fifty to sixty men, most of them Hispanic—though a few Mongolians and Cambodians as well—gather in the parking lot, just outside GT's, waiting for potential employers to drive up, usually in their SUVs, which the laborers swarm to like moths to a lightbulb.

Since it's January, work is hard to come by, which is why these two men were still lingering at the diner at midday. One of them who looked to be in his twenties approached Celikoski and asked for a cigarette. Celikoski gave him one of his Marlboros. "Wake up your friend, please," Celikoski told the young man, who was wearing a GAP baseball cap. The other man, who looked to be in his forties, his hair disheveled, his down jacket ripped, had rested his head on the table. "I wake him up three times," the younger man said. Celikoski calmly walked over to the dozing laborer and gently shook him. "Amigo, wake up. Please, you go home and sleep. Respect me." The man lifted his head, revealing a fresh wound on his forehead. He looked disoriented, as if he'd been drinking. Celikoski walked away, shaking his head. A few days earlier, he told me, feeling sorry for this man, Celikoski had given him a container of chicken noodle soup which he took out on the sidewalk to eat. The man consumed half of it before passing out, falling headfirst into the soup.

Celikoski grumbles incessantly about the day laborers. He says that on occasion they'll leave without paying for their coffee. Do you go after them? I ask. "For seventy-nine cents I say 'forget about it,' " he tells me. He says he's lost customers, especially women and children, who are intimidated by the loitering men. He says they'll gamble on the sidewalk outside, that they'll occasionally get into fights. And he contends they can't find work because they're too greedy. "They ask for too much money," he says. "They ask for one hundred fifty dollars for eight hours. It's no good." But the thing about it is if you spend time at GT's with Celikoski, listening to him try out his newly learned Spanish and offering the recently purchased hot pepper mix, one gets the distinct impression that he rather enjoys their company.

I arrive one morning, shortly after seven a.m. It's thirteen degrees out, and so GT's is packed with the day laborers seeking refuge from the cold. One man, who tells me his name is George and that he arrived from Guatemala fifteen years ago, is sitting at the counter, eating a breakfast of three scrambled eggs, potatoes, toast, and coffee. He's one of the few who actually buys a meal, this one for $3.39, usually when he's just finished a job and is flush with cash. He spent the past two days cleaning an abandoned factory for nine dollars an hour; it was his first hire in twelve days. (Many of the day laborers tell me that they do indeed ask for a lot of money but that it's because they need room to negotiate; otherwise, they say, they run the risk of getting paid near or even below minimum wage.) George is thirty-six and has soft features and an open face. He's wearing a black skullcap that he's shaped into the form of a Robin Hood hat. He taught elementary school in Guatemala, and in his first few years in the United States he worked in a poultry plant in South Carolina before it closed. "He's my friend," he says, nodding at Celikoski, who's flipping a pair of frying eggs. "Juan," he says of Celikoski, "he's kind of a quiet guy. He's trying with his

Spanish. Sometimes I make my order in Spanish." He smiles mischievously. "I'll speak to him in Spanish. See if he understands."

"*Te gustan los tacos?*" George asks.

"*Mucho,*" Celikoski replies.

"*Que tipo de tacos?*"

"*Pollo y carne.*"

"*Bueno,*" George tells Celikoski.

Another customer, Manuel Rodas, also from Guatemala, is at the other end of the counter. He's listening in on the conversation. He tells me that not long ago, he'd arrived one morning after a few days of steady work, and ordered breakfast. He then realized he'd left his wallet at home. Celikoski told him not to worry. He could pay the next day, which he did. Celikoski interrupts. He thanks Rodas for recently fixing the store's toilet handle, which had broken from so much usage. "He tried to pay me but I said no," Rodas tells me. "So he gave me a free meal."

A white man in a leather jacket walks into GT's, seeking workers. He sits down at a booth and is quickly surrounded by ten men. He's looking for someone with a truck, and so the men call out to George, who owns a small battered pickup. George is gone before I can get his last name.

I return a week later, on the Martin Luther King holiday. Celikoski had told me that a group of community organizers planned to hold a press conference at the diner to draw attention to the day laborers' frustration at not having a permanent site. "You agreed to let them hold the press conference at your diner?" I had asked, somewhat incredulous given his previous rant. He shrugged. "It's a slow day for business anyway," he said. When I arrive, the place is packed, maybe thirty people, most of them simply milling around. As people order cups of coffee or hot chocolate, it becomes clear that Celikoski has no intention of taking their money. When he sees there are some children at the rally, he asks one parent how many of them there are. The father looks perplexed. He counts on his fingers. "Eight," he says.

"I make eight egg sandwiches for them," Celikoski insists. "On the house."

At one point, I comment to Celikoski's lone employee, a newly arrived young Albanian, that he's going to give away the restaurant. The young man, as if to mimic his employer, shrugs. "He's the boss," he says. Celikoski later tells me that he doesn't expect to turn a profit until the warm months when the business picks up and the day laborers find construction work and so are gone by early morning.

The next day, Celikoski is grumbling again. "Let me tell you something," he says. "If America has a job for everybody, and these fifty, sixty people don't, maybe they are lazy, maybe they don't want to work. When I come to this country I find a job right away." He then shows me a letter he'd received earlier that day from "concerned residents" (there were no names attached) asking shop owners in the mall to post NO TRESPASSING signs, and to file complaints with the police about the day laborers loitering in the strip mall's parking lot. "Will you?" I ask Celikoski. He shakes his head. "I feel sorry," he tells me. "Some of them are good." He says that as a child in Albania he learned from his parents something called *besa-bes,* which, he tells me, means if someone comes to your home, you help them. "Winter," he says, "it's tough for everybody."

Isn't That the Corniche?

T HIS IS A SHORT AND YET EMBLEMATIC TALE ABOUT
Chicago. At its center is a man who was so in love
with his city's architecture that he decided to find a way to
have it captured on film for posterity. In the course of one
year, he managed to accumulate more than half a million
photographs, but in the end, few of them were of buildings, and even fewer have remained on display in the city
itself, instead ending up in the unlikeliest places.

In 1963 Gary Comer, an unassuming man who had
grown up in Chicago and who had a comfortable position
in advertising, quit his job to pursue his passion: sailing.
He and a friend opened a small mail-order company that
sold hardware for sailboats, and the firm did okay until the
oil embargo of the early 1970s, when powerboat stores,
faced with the decline in sales of their usual wares, mus-
cled in on their sailboat business. So Comer diversified and
began selling other things—first big-brimmed hats, and

then clothing in general. His business took off, in time morphing into what we know today as Lands' End. It became the nation's largest catalogue clothing company, and Comer eventually sold the firm to Sears for $1.9 billion.

Not long ago, in a survey conducted by the American Institute of Architects, its members declared Chicago home to the finest architecture in the country, and Comer and his wife, Francie, would agree; every Sunday they used to take a drive around the city, mostly to admire its older buildings. On one of these drives, in 1999, Comer was approaching the Loop from the south and he suddenly understood that he was watching a city shedding its skin: "I saw this magnificent façade of buildings, and I realized that what I was looking at was temporary. There isn't much over one hundred twenty years old in the city. Most buildings last eighty to a hundred years. I realized the city was really in transition. New buildings going up. Old ones coming down." And in that instant, Comer had a notion. "The city was being rebuilt from the center out. I thought, 'Gee, let's lock it into place at the end of the millennium.'" He decided to hire some photographers to capture the city as it was right at this moment in its history; then he might create a kind of time capsule, perhaps bury it in a canister beneath a new park under construction downtown.

Comer approached Richard Cahan to head up the project. Cahan was a likely candidate for the job because he'd written a book about a local architectural photographer, Richard Nickel, who was among the first preservationists to fight for buildings because of their architectural rather than their historical significance. (In 1972, Nickel died doing what he loved: While he was combing through Chicago's old Stock Exchange, bulldozers bore through the building and buried him.) Cahan, who was also the picture editor at the *Chicago Sun-Times*, told Comer, "If you're going to capture the city you ought to capture its people, its life, not the architecture. That's what people will care about a thousand years from now." Besides, he added, "Human lives are more interesting than buildings." Comer gradually came to agree, and so Cahan left his job at the *Sun-Times* to direct the project, which they christened CITY 2000.

Two hundred local photographers were hired, most of them on a part-time basis, to take pictures around the city over the next year. Comer didn't set a budget; he just told Cahan and the photographers he assembled to make it as good as possible. "I don't want to hear any excuses," he told them. Initially, Cahan skimped. When they needed aerial shots, for instance, he rented an old Piper airplane that cost seventy-five dollars an hour, but the resulting photographs were distant and out of focus. Comer heard of the problem and suggested they hire a turbo helicopter at five hundred twenty-five dollars an hour. In the end, Comer spent roughly two million dollars on the project.

Photographers were given free rein and told to do whatever they'd long dreamed of doing. Leah Missbach asked women throughout the city to empty the contents of their purses, and then shot the contents along with the owners. Lloyd DeGrane took photos of people in uniform, from players for the Chicago Cubs to maids at the Hilton Hotel. Scott Strazzante documented the last days of a tire store where his father worked. Kevin Horan set up a makeshift studio at ten locations around the city, including outside the Criminal Courts building, by the lakefront, and on the streets of Albany Park, and asked passersby if he might photograph them against a white sheet. The result is an arresting collection of everyday people out of context. The subjects' faces, their clothes, their postures reveal all, almost as if you'd caught them in a state of undress: two elderly women in matching pink bathing suits; a bulging defense attorney in a mustard-stained shirt; a musician with his trumpet. Horan asked each subject two questions. The first was, "Why are you here?" The second was, "What would you like people to know about that they wouldn't know from looking at your picture?"—to which one woman, a young model, replied, "That I am really a nice person because everyone thinks I'm a bitch."

So, what to do with all these photographs? For two and a half months they were shown at the city's Cultural Center in the Loop, where they were visited by twenty-five thousand people, a respectable number for exhibitions there. Then the five hundred thousand negatives were collected for storage at the library of the University of Illinois at Chicago. The collection has never found its rightful place in the city.

Both Comer and Cahan have moved on. Comer grew

up on the South Side—his father was a conductor for the Illinois Central Railroad—and during the CITY 2000 year, he visited the elementary school he'd attended. The students are now all African-American, and mostly poor. He asked the principal, "How are they treating you?"

"Beg your pardon?" the principal replied.

"Are you getting everything you need?"

In fact, the principal told Comer, they had new computers that were sitting idle because the school wasn't properly wired. Comer paid to have that done, and he has since made the well-being of the Paul Revere Elementary School an ongoing priority. He has also provided funding for the South Shore Drill Team, whose director is the school's disciplinarian; two hundred fifty kids participate, and there are another hundred on the waiting list. They're a crowd favorite at the Bud Billiken Day Parade. As for Cahan, he opened a store in Evanston, the suburb just north of the city. It's called CityFile, and it sells rare books on Chicago as well as photographs, memorabilia, and original art. Cahan's running out of money, though, and when I last saw him he told me he would probably close soon. But one of his final gestures was to hold an exhibition, the first in the city, of Robert Guinan's work. In Paris, there's a tradition that on weekends artists will drop by their galleries to meet with art-seekers, and so, for a month, Guinan visited Cahan's store each Saturday afternoon and held court. A number of visitors, thinking Guinan lived in Paris, asked him how often he visited Chicago. Another began speaking to him in French. "All I could say is *'Où est le téléphone?'* " he said. "It's the only French I know."

Guinan would undoubtedly identify with the fate of CITY 2000, for the project has resurfaced far from Chicago. In September 2001, the city entered one hundred thirty-five of the photographs in the International Photography Festival in Aleppo, Syria, and the show opened on September 11—the day the world's axis shifted. Valentine Judge, who works for the city and was traveling with the exhibition, told the Syrians that "in these pictures you see the faces of the fathers, mothers, sisters, and brothers of the people killed in the World Trade Center. This is what America looks like." People were drawn to the photographs, which were the hit of the festival, and so the U.S. State Department chose to take these images of Chicago around the world—more precisely, to the places where America is viewed with some hostility. So far they have been exhibited in India, Lebanon, Egypt, Morocco, Tunisia, South Africa, Brazil, Jordan, Thailand, and Malaysia. The pictures continue to make their way around the globe.

People, after all, like looking at people, and peeking in at American life. A photograph of a rather large woman in a body-clinging dress often gets puzzled looks, presumably because obesity is not a common sight in most Third World countries. Passersby look on in amusement at a diptych of a woman in a North Side bar called Slow Down Life's Too Short and the emptied contents of her purse, which include a disposable camera, an address book, a pack of Marlboro Lights, a cell phone, a makeup case, a wallet, keys (to her motorcycle, car, bike lock, and apartment), a credit card, and sunglasses—the daily accoutrements of life in America. There are portraits of two waitresses, one with a nose ring, at the South Side restaurant Soul Queen; a group of Ethiopian Jews celebrating the Sabbath; two Mexican-Americans dancing at a rodeo in Pilsen; four Knights of Columbus members dressed in feathered fezzes, capes, and sashes; and Rex, a toothless, smiling homeless man in a Laborers' Union baseball cap.

But people also see themselves in these photos: an entire world reflected in one place, in one city. In Beirut, a woman looking at an image of two veiled Muslim women standing by Lake Michigan asked, "Isn't that the Corniche?" In Bombay, a cleaning woman in her sari took Judge's hand and walked her over to a picture of a nine-year-old girl about to be baptized at the Unity of Love Missionary Baptist Church on the city's South Side; she pointed first to the shower-cap-clad girl, and then to herself. An Indian diplomat translated: "She's trying to tell you she's Christian. That she was baptized." In Tunis, a middle-aged man looking at an image of a young Puerto Rican man with his wife's name, Natalie, shaved into his hair, mumbled, "Oh, I hope my son doesn't see that." One of the favorites is from Horan's collection, a portrait of two teenage friends on their way home from school: One girl is a Somali, wearing a traditional head scarf, and the other is from Thailand.

For Cahan, the project had from the beginning seemed

like an opportunity to freeze-frame America, and what better place to do that than in Chicago. Ordered and bedraggled. Excessive and austere. Familiar and foreign. An imperfect city, a city of quixotic quests and of reluctant resignation. A city that was, Algren once wrote, the product "of Man's endless war against himself." These are Chicago's truths but they are also, after all, America's truths, and they always have been.

I've heard it suggested that Chicago is passé. The steel mills have closed. Public housing is coming down. The mob has been dismantled. And, Chicago is no longer hog butcher to the world. Even the city's one claim to edginess, *Playboy* magazine, has picked up shop and moved. "I love Chicago," the magazine's new editor who's now based in New York told a reporter. "It's my second favorite city." The city, though, always finds a way to move on: Now, for example, with more than a hundred sweets manufacturers, it has become the world's candy capital. (As I write, two large confectioners have announced their closing; it is, indeed, a city in motion.)

When Comer first considered his project, it was because he'd been struck by the vast physical changes here, but in the end, what he captured was a people—a people evolving, a people shifting and changing, a people finding their way. I asked Comer why he thought the photographs of Chicago had become such an attraction abroad. "Because," he replied simply, "the place is real."

Acknowledgments

THANKS TO Tony Fitzpatrick, Kale Williams, Andrew Patner, Nancy Drew, Julie Aimen, Isabel Wilkerson, Rachel Reinwald, John Houston, Dan Kotlowitz, Melissa Fay Greene, Amy Dorn, and my wife's family. A grateful nod to *This American Life* and *The Atlantic,* where I had told much of the Cicero story before, and to Chicago Public Radio, where I first told of meeting Milton Reed. Of course, with gratitude and for their patience: Ed Sadlowski, Millie Wortham, Brenda Stephenson, Milton Reed, Andrea Lyon, Bob Guinan, John Celikoski, and Dave Boyle.

Thanks to my friends Alice Truax, who, with her usual grace and exactness, nudged me when my storytelling was out of whack; Kevin Horan, who kept me from going off half-cocked; and Tim Samuelson, who kept me from getting it wrong. (Any errors, of course, are my own doing.) And to Studs Terkel, whose friendship and work has inspired.

To Doug Pepper, for asking—and for seeing it through with such care and good cheer. It's a better book for it. And to David Black, my agent and good friend, for making it happen, as always.

Finally, to my father, Bob Kotlowitz, for all good things. And to my beloved wife, Maria, who keeps me real.

About the Author

ALEX KOTLOWITZ is the author of *The Other Side of the River* and *There Are No Children Here,* which the New York Public Library named as one of the most important books of the twentieth century. A former staff writer at the *Wall Street Journal,* his work has appeared in *The New York Times Magazine* and *The New Yorker,* as well as on *This American Life* and PBS. He has received the George Foster Peabody Award, the Robert F. Kennedy Journalism Award, and the George Polk Award. He is a writer-in-residence at Northwestern University and a visiting professor at the University of Notre Dame.

Chicago Neighborhoods

Key to front endpaper map